BELLY DANCING

BELLY DANCING

Tina Hobin

with photographs by
Kristyna K'ashvili

Duckworth

Third impression 1998

First published in 1982 by
Gerald Duckworth & Co. Ltd
The Old Piano Factory
48 Hoxton Square, London N1 6PB

ISBN 0 7156 1605 6 (paper)

British Library Cataloguing in Publication Data

Hobin, Tina
   Belly Dancing.
   1. Belly dance
   I. Title
   793.3'2   GV1798

ISBN 0-7156-1605-6

Photoset in North Wales by
Derek Doyle & Associates, Mold, Clwyd
Printed in Great Britain by
Redwood Books, Trowbridge, Wiltshire

How graceful are your feet in sandals,
  O queenly maiden!
Your rounded thighs are like jewels,
  the work of a master hand.
Your navel is a rounded bowl
  that never lacks mixed wine.
Your belly is a heap of wheat,
  encircled with lilies.

Song of Solomon 7.1-2

Contents

Introduction

Belly dancing is no longer confined to the world of burning sand and the equally burning passions of the harem — it is spreading through the western world as a unique and exciting way of keeping fit and at the same time adding a new zest to life.

Belly dancing is now being recognised as a skilful physical art form, which combines health-giving exercise with the creative grace of dance movements and a degree of exhilaration and relaxation second to none.

For years the West has looked to oriental mysticism for spiritual guidance and relaxation. Now it is beginning to discover and appreciate the physical and emotional revitalisation which comes from this oriental dance.

Belly dancing evolved originally from a combination of symbolic rituals and sexual stimulation; the callisthenic aspect was incidental rather than fundamental. In its new role as a healthy physical art form, the emphasis is on its keep-fit qualities. That it is also sexually exciting is in the nature of a bonus.

All dancing is a means of communication: between dancers, between the dancer and the audience, and between the dancer's physical and mental selves. There is an element of the exhibitionist in most of us — whatever form it may take — and belly dancing offers a perfect opportunity to create your own fantasies.

Like other forms of dance, belly dancing is a wonderful medium for individual interpretation and role playing. Once you have become thoroughly familiar with all the steps, you no longer need to plan your movements consciously and you can afford to let your imagination have full rein. This is where you can push your everyday image into the background and let your hidden urges take over.

The awareness of your new mental and emotional liberation will enable your movements to be naturally graceful and fluid, so that your undulating rhythms and uninhibited vitality will turn the wheel full circle and enable your body and mind to derive the greatest possible benefit.

Feminists need have no fear that belly dancing suggests subservience, or in any way undermines their sexual equality. On the contrary, it encourages and develops strength, initiative and confidence, which can all be used to full advantage in any situation.

And don't forget the man in your life! By the time you have progressed sufficiently to introduce him to the 'new you', he will be delighted. Belly dancing will do as much for him as it will for you.

Correct exercise, undertaken in reasonable amounts, is good, physically and mentally, for everyone — irrespective of age. Just as babies and children need plenty of exercise for sturdy development, so adults need to continue with appropriate exercise in order to maintain fitness, to lessen fatigue and to develop an overall feeling of well-being.

Lack of exercise is a common cause of overweight, bad circulation, poor sleeping, breathlessness, weak muscles, stiff joints and premature aging. This is why belly dancing constitutes such an ideal form of exercise. Its wide range of graduated physical exercises is designed to tone up the whole body, while the creative potential of the dance steps stimulates and relaxes.

It is also an excellent form of therapy for tension and depression. A student in her mid-thirties, who had suffered from colitis for many years, was highly delighted that her problem (which had been diagnosed as a stress condition) completely disappeared when she started attending classes regularly. Once you have learned the basic dance steps, you can give full rein to your creative abilities as you evolve your own individual dance interpretations. This 'mental holiday' enables you to ease all your tensions, so that you feel both invigorated and relaxed.

Muscles work in groups and become stronger through use; when they are idle, they become weak and have to be retrained to function effectively. If you discipline your muscles steadily to their full capacity you will learn to move different parts of your body quite independently from others, and you may be surprised to find that you are getting responses from muscles you never knew you had. There are approximately 650 muscles in the body, working in groups – one contracting while another relaxes – and so allowing the joints to move.

When muscles lose their strength and firmness they become flabby. Daily exercise will help to maintain muscle tone and strength, improving posture and health in general.

Correct posture is important. Incorrect posture, such as rounded shoulders and head jutting forward, can cause muscle strain due to imbalance in the body. Backache and many other discomforts may follow. When you are standing correctly your chest should be elevated, your stomach pulled in, and your head held erect.

While belly dancing works wonders for your health and general well-being, it also has the effect of enhancing your sex life in many subtle ways. As you gradually progress through the exercises and dances, you shake off all sorts of unwanted inhibitions and hang-ups. You become aware of your newly acquired confidence, vitality and suppleness. These combine to heighten love-making for yourself and your partner, and this can bring a new dimension of communication and pleasure to your relationship.

Diet

Much of the effort you put into your various exercises will be wasted if you counterbalance it with wrong eating habits. A sensible diet and exercise complement each other, so that you get the full benefit of both.

There is a wealth of material already written about diets of every kind, but it is worth keeping in mind the fundamental structure of a well-balanced diet.

We tend to associate malnutrtion with the so-called Third World, but ironically the rise in our own standard of living in affluent countries does not mark an equivalent rise in nutritional standards. We are presented with an abundance of pre-packed, over-refined convenience foods which may tempt many of us to eat too much – and worse, to eat too much of the wrong kind of food, which is high in calories (and therefore fattening), but low in nutrients.

Unless they are on a special medically prescribed diet, most people can achieve a wise pattern of eating by following a few simple principles: (a) foods with a high animal-fat, refined starch or sugar content, fried foods and 'stodge' should be kept to a minimum; (b) eggs, cottage cheese, cream-free milk, yoghurt, lean meat, fish, poultry and nuts provide the necessary protein and calcium and should form a moderate part of the daily intake; (c) a balanced diet should include an adequate amount of natural fibre, and this is best supplied by whole-grain products such as wholemeal bread and flour, bran and wholewheat cereals, which also contain important vitamins; (d) the other major group consists of the green vegetables and fruits (especially beneficial when eaten raw) which supply various kinds of fibre, health-giving vitamins and minerals. Foods in this last group may be eaten in greater quantities, particularly if you are feeling hungry, as their lower calorie content makes them less fattening.

(I am grateful to Sue Bacon for providing information on diet.)

Ghawazee dancing girls

1 *The History of Belly Dancing*

There have been many theories about the origin of belly dancing, but most evidence links it to the Middle East and Africa. Some say it was originated by the Phoenicians; others claim that it was introduced into Egypt by the Turks. Egyptian tomb paintings from as far back as the fourteenth century BC depict partially clad dancers whose callisthenic positions appear to be very similar to those used in belly dancing.

Anthropologists have recorded many types of tribal dances performed specifically as a prelude to sexual stimulation and initiation rites, courtship displays and fertility rituals. To many primitive societies living close to nature, the undulating movements of the pelvis and abdomen, involving muscular control, were symbolic enactments of both conception and birth and constituted an essential part of their religion and way of life. When a woman was giving birth, she would adopt a squatting position, bearing down as she moved her abdomen in a rolling motion, which assisted birth.

In Africa and Polynesia dancers of both sexes would gyrate their hips and breasts in an endless variety of postures, to an ecstatic rhythmic beat which developed into a complete erotic dance.

In India the symbolic movement of the dancers was not only an art but an act of worship. On Indian shrines and on a thirteenth-century temple wall at Konarak, Hindu dancing girls carved in stone are depicted in various erotic postures similar to those employed in belly dancing.

Good dancers had incredible muscle control – every gesture and posture included the whole body, each movement being a significant expression of love towards the gods. Not surprisingly the dance became rather more erotic than spiritual. Many of the temple dancers became debauched, turning to prostitution, and were banished from the temples.

Two great centres of ancient dancing were the town of Cadiz in Spain and the river Nile in Egypt. The expression of the dance was in the individual dancers' body movements. The transparent garments worn by the dancers were frequently discarded. In Egypt the tradition and skills of the dance have changed little through fifty centuries, and as in ancient Egypt the garments worn have always been a negligible element of the art.

The dancing girls of Egypt from the Ghawazee tribe performed unveiled in the public streets to amuse the rabble. Their dancing had little elegance. The dancers would begin decorously enough, but soon their movements became more energetic and more vibrant, in time with the rapid rhythmic beat of the cymbals. They often performed in the court of a house or in the street in front of a house, on festive occasions in the harem, such as a marriage or the birth of a child. The Ghawazee dancing girls were never admitted into a respectable harem, but they were frequently hired to entertain a party of men in a house of ill repute. These performances were more lascivious and they usually wore nothing but the *smintiyan* (trousers) or a very full skirt called a *tob*.

The dress that was generally worn in

public was very similar to that worn by the middle-class women of Egypt in private. The dancers also wore various ornaments and bordered their eyes with *kohl*. The palms of their hands and their toes and feet were usually stained red with henna, according to the custom of the upper classes of Egyptian women.

Many people of Cairo persuaded themselves that there was nothing improper in the dancing of the Ghawazee, but the fact that it was performed by females who ought not to expose themselves led men to dance in the same manner. They were mostly young men and boys called Khawals, Muslims and natives of Egypt. Their dress consisted chiefly of a tight vest, a girdle and a kind of petticoat. They let their hair grow long and braided it in the manner of the women, and also imitated the women in applying kohl to their eyes, and henna to their feet. In the streets, when they were not engaged in dancing, they would often veil their faces to affect the manners of the women. They were frequently employed in preference to the Ghawazee, to dance in front of a house or in its court on the occasion of a marriage, birth or circumcision, and often performed at popular festivals.

In Cairo there was another class of male dancer whose performances, dress and general appearance were similar to that of the Khawals. Generally they were Jews, Armenians, Greeks and Turks, who were distinguished by a different appelation – *gink* – a Turkish term that had vulgar significance.

In Egypt the belly dance is still very much part of folklore and tradition. Men still dance at social functions, including weddings. In contrast to the undulating movements of the women the male dance involves much turning and leaping, and includes the use of sticks. Other male dancers, usually soloists, perform an exhilarating hip shimmy to the beat of a drum.

The *danse du ventre* (literally belly dance) of Turkish origin was introduced to Paris by Turkish women. They exhibited it in Midway Plaisance of the Colombian Exposition in Chicago in 1893, and then at the California Midwinter Exposition in San Francisco. As performed by Turkish women, the dance consists of control and movements of the abdominal and chest muscles; hence its other name 'muscle dance'. Varied with graceful steps and gyrations, cymbals and scarves, it was performed solo, accompanied by male Turkish musicians with Turkish instruments.

A dance closely associated with it, of a wholly independent religious origin, is the hula hula dance of Hawaiian women. It is possibly less energetic and abandoned than the Turkish dance.

The Americans and other western women learned belly dancing from the Turks and Egyptians, but their versions are often less graceful and subtle than the original, possibly because of their more puritanical attitude towards the dance. This is something you may have to combat when learning to belly dance; but when you have overcome these feelings, you will be well on the way to being a good dancer.

2 *Music and Instruments*

Middle Eastern music has definite rhythmic patterns; the rhythms are uncomplicated and the belly dance is improvised – a visual expression and interpretation of the rhythms. The musicians improvise too, their moods and speed changing dramatically from lively tempos to slow, dramatic and intense ones.

You will probably need to listen many times to various records before you become familiar with the different rhythms, beats and moods that Middle Eastern music portrays. The dancer expresses her personality through her movements, changing her mood dramatically from happy to tense and then back again to happy.

The music is divided into two sections: the *tchefetetelli* and the *taxim*. The tchefetetelli is sometimes referred to as the *belida*, an Arabic word referring to the lively part of the dance. The musicians play happy, lively music with a combination of instruments, varying in tempo from slow to medium to fast.

The predominant beat is basically four-count, 1-2-3-4, which is played slower (slowed down) or much faster, doubling the beat of four counts to 1 and 2 and 3 and 4, the accent being on the first and third beat. 9/8 rhythm is three beats of two counts and one beat of three counts, the accent being on the 1-3-5-7 beats, as follows:

1 2 3 4 5 6 7 8 9

Other rhythms, such as 7/8, 6/8 and 5/4 are more complicated and a little difficult for the beginner to follow.

The drum constantly beats out the varying rhythm. Therefore listen carefully to the drum beat and changes of rhythm, tapping out the beat with your *zills* (finger cymbals – see Chapter 5), fingers or foot.

The belly dancer makes her entrance on to the floor at the beginning of the tchefetetelli or belida section, spinning and turning around the floor, creating an atmosphere. During this section you can use some of your basic dance movements, such as hip rotations, pelvic rolls and abdominal rolls. During the slower tempo of the tchefetetelli rhythm vary your combination of movements using your veil. If the music changes tempo before you have finished your veil routine, you can extend it to the next section of music. When you have come to the end of your veil routine, drop your veil gracefully to the floor, or move towards the audience, shimmying seductively, and drape the veil around the neck of some friendly spectator.

As the tchefetetelli speeds up, the dance movements become more abandoned and exhilarating. During these fast combinations of dance steps vary your routine by using the zills.

In complete contrast to the tchefetetelli rhythm is the taxim section. Here the musicians play an improvised solo, invariably making use of the *ood* or clarinet, both of which produce a soulful wailing sound. This section is played much more slowly and is more dramatic and intense. As the taxim begins, descend to the floor gracefully, and sensually perform the floor movements with a few slow movements, such as hip rotations and figure-eights, until the music changes to a livelier tempo.

There are various ancient Middle Eastern

instruments, of which the most typical are the *ood, nay, darabukkeh, kanoon, santeer* and *kemengeh*. Other instruments used are the more popularly known ones such as the clarinet, violin, bazooki and tambourine. The more familiar you become with Middle Eastern music the more easily you will be able to pick out and identify the various sounds of the musical instruments.

I will now describe the instruments which are not so well known in the West. Man-made materials may have replaced some of the substances traditionally used in the manufacture of these instruments.

The *darabukkeh* is a kind of drum. It is placed under the left arm and suspended by a cord which passes over the left shoulder. It is beaten with both hands, and makes a different sound according to whether it is struck near the edge or in the middle. The best darabukkeh is fifteen inches long, made of wood and covered in mother of pearl. A more common type is made of clay, but differs little in form – it is covered with a piece of fish skin at the larger end and is open at the smaller end. The clay drum can be up to two feet long, and is mainly used in the harems.

The *kemengeh* is approximately thirty inches long. The soundboard (which is the flat part of the body) is made from part of a coconut, which is pierced with many small soundholes. The front is covered with a piece of fish skin, on which rests the bridge. The neck is cylindrical and made of ebony, inlaid with ivory; at the base there is also a piece of ivory. The pegs themselves, which are used to tune the strings, are made of beech, and their heads are of ivory. The foot, which is made of iron, passes through the soundboard and is inserted into the neck of the instrument up to a depth of three inches. Each chord consists of about sixty horse hairs, which are attached to an iron ring below the soundboard towards the other end. Each is lengthened with a

The *kemengeh*

piece of lamb's gut attaching it to its peg. Over the chords, just below this point, is a double band of leather, which is tied around the neck of the instrument. The bow is about thirty-four inches long and is generally made of ash. Horse hairs pass through a hole at the end of the bow, where they are secured by a knot. At the other end they are attached by an iron ring, which is tightened or slackened by a band of leather passing through the iron ring and through a second ring at the base of the bow.

The *kanoon*, a stringed instrument, is made partly of walnut. Its face and back are made of deal, a soft wood. The bridge, the sides and the piece in which the pegs are inserted are made of beech, as is the ridge along its interior edge through which the chords pass. The pegs are of poplar. In the central part of the instrument's face is a circular piece of wood pierced with holes. Towards the acute angle of the face is another similar piece of wood pierced with holes. In the part of the face the bridge rests on there are five oblong openings, corresponding with the five feet of the bridge. A piece of fish skin nine inches wide is glued over this part and the five feet of the bridge rests upon those parts of skin which cover the five openings, slightly depressing the skin. There are three chords to each note – twenty treble chords in all – made of lamb's gut. The shortest side of the instrument is veneered with walnut and inlaid with mother of pearl. The instrument is played with two plectrums made of buffalo horn attached to the forefinger of each hand, and it rests on the musician's knees when played.

The *dulcimer*, more commonly known as the *santeer*, is very similar to the kanoon, except that it has two sides equally tapering together, instead of one; and it has double

The *kanoon*

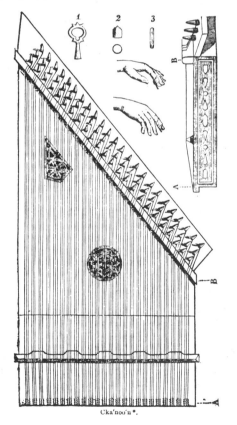

Cka'noo'u *.

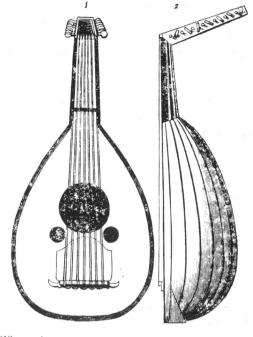

The *ood*

chords made of wire instead of treble chords of lamb's gut. These are struck with two small hammers or mallets.

The *ood* is a lute (the original meaning of *ood* is 'flexible stick'). For many centuries it was commonly used by the best Arab musicians, and has been celebrated by many poets. It is played with a plectrum, and is approximately twenty-five inches long. The body is made of deal, and the edges and neck faced with ebony. On the face there are three circular pieces of ebony, one large and two small, which are pierced with small holes, to which a piece of fish skin is glued. This prevents the wood from being torn away by the plectrum. There are seven double strings, two to each note, made of lamb's gut.

The *nay*, a wind instrument, is a kind of flute. It is a reed approximately eighteen inches long, one inch in diameter at the upper end and three-quarters of an inch at the lower end. There are six holes in the front and usually another at the back.

There are two other types of reed pipe. One is the double reed pipe called a *zummarah*. The other, in which one pipe is much longer than the other, is called an *arghool*. This has a bass sound and is just over three feet long. The arghool has three moveable pieces to lengthen the longer tube, and is sometimes used with only two of these, or with neither.

The *bazooki* is a stringed instrument very similar to a lute or mandolin. The strings are metal and are played with a plectrum, producing a metallic sound.

1. & 2. Earthen *darabukkeh*
3. & 4. *Zummarah*
5. Extension pipe for the *arghool*
6. *Arghool*

3　The Exercises

How to begin

If you haven't been in the habit of exercising, begin in easy stages, stopping if you become breathless or feel aches and pains other than those you might naturally feel when you start using muscles which have hitherto been idle.

Similarly, if you are middle-aged, and generally out of condition, and if you suffer from backache or have had any recent operations or injuries, *check with your doctor before you start*.

Ideally, belly dancing classes, where training can be given by an expert, are the best place to learn. The group atmosphere provides companionship and plenty of laughter, as well as speeding the learning process. However, for various reasons not every enthusiast can attend classes, and it is quite possible for anyone to learn at home, if the step-by-step lessons and detailed instructions in this book are followed carefully. But don't expect to become an expert belly dancer in a week. It is an art which takes time and practice to perfect.

Whether you are able to join a class or whether you decide to begin at home, all the exercises and dance steps which follow have been designed systematically, to be carried out in strict sequence, each one leading on naturally to the next.

If you are practising at home, choose a room with as much space as possible and preferably with a full-length mirror. If you have to use a smaller mirror, arrange its height so that you can observe your abdomen and hips, and so ensure that you are making the correct movements.

Suitable practice attire is obviously necessary. You don't need to buy special clothing just to do the exercises, but choose something unrestricting and comfortable, such as a leotard, swimsuit or bra and briefs. The important thing is to allow your body complete freedom of movement.

If at first it suits you better to break your practice time into two or three shorter spells, try to arrange your clothing so that you can slip the top layers on and off with the minimum amount of time and trouble.

It is a good idea to limit your practice sessions to ten minutes at first, to allow your body to adjust without undue strain, and then gradually to increase the time as you start to loosen up and are able to make full use of all your muscles in a properly co-ordinated way.

The programme of correct breathing and graduated exercises which follows enables you to tone up your whole body and improve your figure dramatically. At the same time it is probably the most pleasant and simple aid to slimming.

Correct breathing

You may find it difficult to breathe correctly at first, as it is the reverse of the way many of us normally interpret 'deep breathing'.

The essence of correct deep breathing is to exercise the diaphragm (the muscular partition between the chest and abdomen) so that, when you breathe in, its dome-like shape 'flattens', thereby enlarging the chest cavity to enable you to take in the maximum amount of air. This pushes the abdominal organs down, causing the abdomen to swell. Then, as you pull your tummy in, the diaphragm is raised again and this helps you to expel the stale air from your lungs. Thus, when you develop a correct breathing routine, you increase your oxygen supply, stimulate your blood circulation and strengthen flabby abdominal muscles.

If you persevere regularly with the correct breathing routine and make a determined effort to improve your posture at the same time, these two vital ingredients for health and beauty will eventually become an automatic part of your daily routine whatever you are doing.

(a) Stand with your feet about 12 inches apart: i.e. in line with your hips
(b) *Contract:* pull in your stomach, tightening the abdominal muscles
(c) *Elevate:* lift your rib cage and push out
(d) *Flex:* bend your knees slightly
(e) *Exhale:* breathe out steadily, emptying your lungs completely (if you place the palms of your hands lightly on your stomach as you exhale, you should be able to feel your diaphragm rising).

The starting position

The position adopted when breathing correctly is the correct starting position, unless otherwise stated, for all the exercises that follow. Whenever you are asked to assume the starting position, you should stand with your feet slightly apart, flex your knees and elevate your rib cage. Exercises 5, 6 and 8 below elaborate on the starting position and correct method of breathing, and you should perform them in the correct sequence, as you will be able to do them more easily once you have loosened up with the preceding exercises.

(1)

Standing exercises

EXERCISE 1 – SIDE STRETCH
These stretching exercises will tone your whole body, making it more flexible from toes to fingertips, improving balance, co-ordination and posture. Perform them slowly and smoothly.

(a) Elevate your rib cage. Raise your arms above your head.
(b) Place your right foot forward (1), keeping your leg straight, and raise the heel.

(2)   (3)   (4)

(c) Slowly stretch the whole of your right side from toes to fingertips. (If you are doing this correctly, you should feel your pelvis pulling down and away from your rib cage).

(d) Relax, placing your right leg beside your left leg. Place your left foot forward (2) and raise the heel, slowly stretch your left side.

(e) Repeat on alternate sides, doing four stretches in all.

EXERCISE 2 – ALTERNATE SIDE STRETCHING

(a) Elevate your rib cage.

(b) Raise your arms above your head.

(c) Place your right foot forward (3), keeping your leg straight, and raise the heel.

(d) Stretch your right leg and at the same time stretch your left arm.

(e) Repeat, stretching your left leg and right arm (4).

(f) Do three or four on each side.

(5)

(6)

EXERCISE 3 – LIMB AND BODY STRETCHING

(a) Assume the starting position but keep your legs straight
(b) Bend forward, arms held out in front with your head between your arms (5).
(c) Stretch your body forward as far as possible without losing your balance. Hold, count up to five.
(d) Bringing your arms down, stand upright. Relax and repeat.

(7)

(8)

EXERCISE 4 – LIMB AND BODY STRETCH VARIATION

(a) Assume the starting position but keep your legs straight.

(b) Bend forward, arms held out in front and head between your arms (5).

(c) Stretch your body forward.

(d) Bring your right arm down, slowly pushing it up and out behind you (6). Then swing your arm up and over (7) to the starting position, completing a full circular movement with your arm (8). Repeat with the left arm.

(e) Continue the exercise, using your arms alternately. Repeat the movement about 20 times, and relax.

(9)   (10)

EXERCISE 5 – FOR THE RIB CAGE

This is a very important exercise used in preparation for most of the dance movements and some exercises.

    (a) Stand with your feet slightly apart.

    (b) Clasp your hands behind your back, resting them lightly on your buttocks (9).

    (c) Contract your tummy muscles, tighten your buttocks.

    (d) Elevate your rib cage by lifting it up and pushing outwards.

    (e) Push your chest and chin forward, stretching your arms back at the same time (10). You should feel your rib cage pulling up and away from the abdomen. Hold, count up to five, relax and repeat.

EXERCISE 6 – BREATHING

(a) Place the palms of your hands lightly on your stomach, just above your waistline.

(b) Count as far as you can without taking a deep breath, and feel your diaphragm rising.

EXERCISE 7 – ABDOMINAL FLUTTER

(a) Stand with your feet slightly apart and your legs straight.

(b) Exhale deeply, and hold your breath.

(c) Bend forward with your arms held out in front of you, and your head between your arms.

(d) Slowly push out your tummy, then pull it in, as many times as you can.

(e) Stand upright, relax and breathe normally, then repeat.

When you can do this exercise without any effort, push your tummy out and pull it in as fast as you can while breathing normally.

EXERCISE 8 – STARTING POSITION

Now is the time to perfect the correct starting position, which is assumed at the beginning of some of the exercises and most dance movements. This will be easier once you have mastered the elevation of the rib cage (Exercise 5). If you are doing it correctly, there should be no effort or strain.

(a) Stand with your feet slightly apart.

(b) Distribute your weight evenly on both legs. Flex your knees.

(c) Contract the abdomen.

(d) Elevate the rib cage.

(e) Relax and repeat.

EXERCISE 9 – THE ABDOMINAL LIFT*

This is an excellent exercise for trimming the waistline, toning tummy muscles and massaging internal organs, and should be done as often as you can throughout the day.

* Exercises 9 and 10 are most easily performed while bending very slightly forward from the hips.

Don't do it if you have just eaten a heavy meal, as it may cause discomfort.

(a) Assume the starting position.

(b) Pushing the tummy out as far as possible, exhale deeply and hold.

(c) Pull your tummy in and up as far as you can. (If you are doing this correctly, you should have a hollow under your rib cage.)

(d) Still with breath held, push your tummy out slowly. Then again pull in and up as far as you can.

(e) Do five abdominal lifts while still holding your breath.

(f) Relax, breathe normally, and then repeat.

EXERCISE 10 – THE ABDOMINAL ROLL*

When you have practiced the abdominal lift, you should be able to roll the abdomen from top to bottom. This exercise needs concentration and may take several weeks or months to perfect. If you practice in front of a mirror you will be able to see whether you are performing the movement correctly.

(a) Assume the starting position, feet slightly apart.

(b) Elevate the rib cage.

(c) Exhale deeply and push your tummy out.

(d) Inhale deeply, pulling your tummy in and up as far as you can. (If you are doing this correctly, you should have a hollow under your rib cage).

(e) Holding this position, push your tummy out and then down, exhaling slowly.

(f) Pull your tummy in and up. Push your tummy out and down.

Eventually you should be able to do many continuous rolls while breathing normally. The abdominal roll is a slow undulating movement which is used many times during the dance routine.

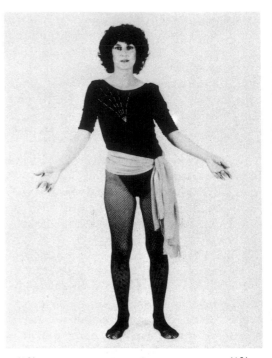

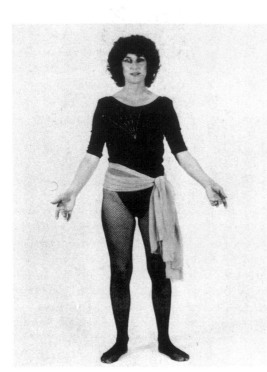

(12) ∧   ∨ (13)

(11)

EXERCISE 11 – RIB CAGE ISOLATION
In this exercise you 'isolate' the muscles so that your rib cage can move independently of the rest of your body.

   (a) Assume the starting position.

   (b) Contract your abdomen, tighten your buttocks and elevate your rib cage.

   (c) Hold your arms out to the side (11).

   (d) Pull your rib cage to the right (12), then pull it to the left (13).

   (e) Keep your shoulders down, and be careful not to twist or move anything other than your rib cage.

   (f) Repeat several times.

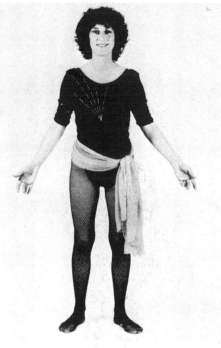

(15) ∧   ∨ (16)

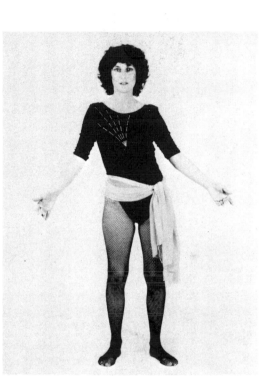

(14)

EXERCISE 12 – RIB CAGE CIRCULATION

(a) Start by performing Exercise 6, from (a) to (c).

(b) Then, in one continuous movement, make a complete circle with your rib cage by pushing it to the right (14), and then forward (15), and then over to the left (16), and then pulling it back.

(17)

(18) ∧   ∨ (19)

EXERCISE 13 – UPPER BODY CIRCULATION

(a) Elevate your rib cage. Place your hands on your hips and stand with your feet slightly apart.

(b) Bend to the right (17). Swing the upper part of your body down and round the front (18) to the left (19). As you straighten up from the left, arch your back (20), continuing the circular movement to the right.

(c) Do four or five to the right. Then repeat the movement doing four in the opposite direction.

Floor Exercises

EXERCISE 14 – ONE SIDE STRETCH
  (a) Lie flat on your back, extending your arms behind your head, with legs together and out straight.

  (b) Slowly stretch your left side only from your toes to your fingertips (21).

  (c) Hold, count up to five, relax and then repeat, stretching the right side.

  (d) Do four stretches in all.

EXERCISE 15 – ALTERNATE SIDE STRETCH
  (a) Lie flat on your back. Extend your arms behind your head, with your legs together and out straight.

  (b) Stretch your right leg and left arm at the same time.

  (c) Hold, count up to five, and relax.

  (d) Stretch your left leg and right arm.

  (e) Do two stretches on each side.

(20)

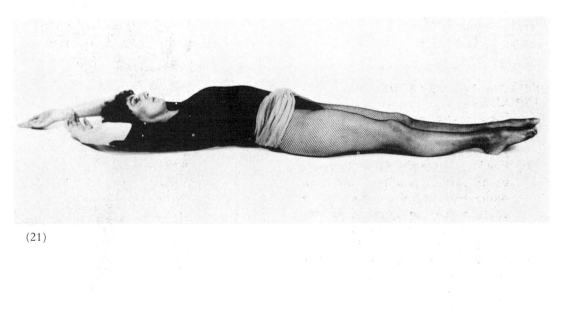

(21)

(22)

(23)

EXERCISE 16 – THE BODY LIFT

(a) Lie flat on your back, legs together and out straight. Extend your arms behind your head.

(b) Arch your body up from the floor, supporting it only with your shoulders and heels (do not raise your head), and stretch slowly (22).

(c) Relax, lowering your body to the floor (23).

(d) Repeat two or three times.

EXERCISE 17 – THE CRESCENT

(a) Lie on your right side with your arms extended behind your head.

(b) Draw your knees up under your chin (24).

(c) Slowly stretch the whole of your body (25), arching your back (including your arms, legs and head) so as to form a bow shape with your body (26).

(d) Hold, count up to five, draw up knees, relax arms, count up to five, then repeat.

(e) Do three of these stretches on one side, roll over, and repeat on the left side.

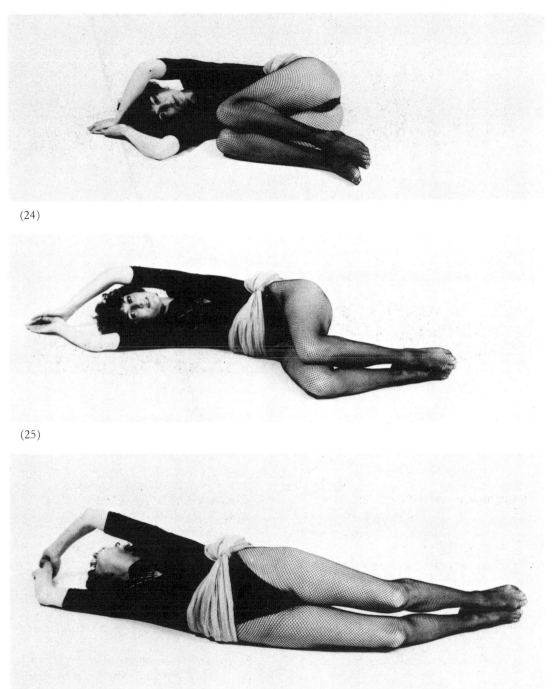

(24)

(25)

(26)

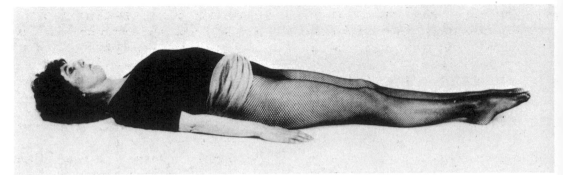

(27)

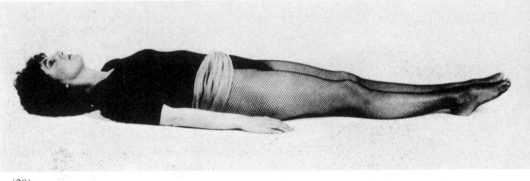

(28)

EXERCISE 18 – PELVIC THRUST

   (a) Lie flat on your back with your arms by your sides, palms up, legs together and out straight.

   (b) Tighten your buttocks, lift your bottom off the floor, thrusting your pelvis up.

   (c) Lower your bottom, pushing your buttocks down on to the floor.

   (d) Repeat ten times.

EXERCISE 19 – FOR THE RIB CAGE

   (a) Lie flat on your back with your arms by your side, legs together and out straight.

   (b) Lift your rib cage (27), pushing it up from the floor.

   (c) Relax, lowering the rib cage (28).

   (d) Repeat several times.

EXERCISE 20 – LEG STRENGTHENING (1)

(a) Lie flat on your tummy and make yourself comfortable. Keep your legs together and out straight.

(b) Curl your toes under and leave them in this position throughout the exercise (29).

(c) Lift your legs up from the floor and stretch (30). Count up to five.

(d) Relax your legs, lowering them to the floor. Repeat ten times, relax and then repeat a further ten times.

EXERCISE 21 – LEG STRENGTHENING (2)

(a) Sit up on the floor with your legs extended in front of you.

(b) Pull your feet up towards you.

(c) Stretch your legs, at the same time pushing the backs of your knees down on to the floor. If you are doing this correctly, your heels should rise slightly from the floor.

(d) Repeat ten times, relax and then repeat a further ten times.

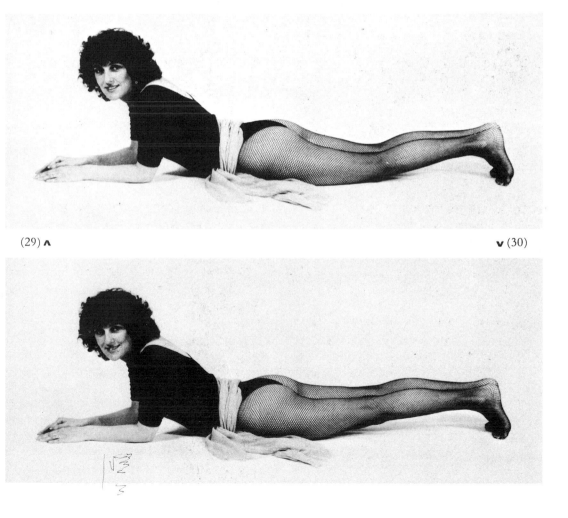

(29) ∧   ∨ (30)

(31)

(32)

EXERCISE 22 – FELINE PRESS UP

(a) Kneel on the floor, bend forward and place your hands on the floor in front of you, keeping your arms straight (31).

(b) Push your rib cage out, contract your tummy.

(c) Tighten the buttocks, and at the same time slowly push the pelvis forward. Bend your arms and lower your chest to the floor (32).

(d) Come up slowly (33), straightenir your arms, pushing your bottom u and arching your back (34) as you c so.

(e) Relax the abdomen, buttocks and r cage (35), hold to the count of fiv and then repeat, doing it as mar times as you can.

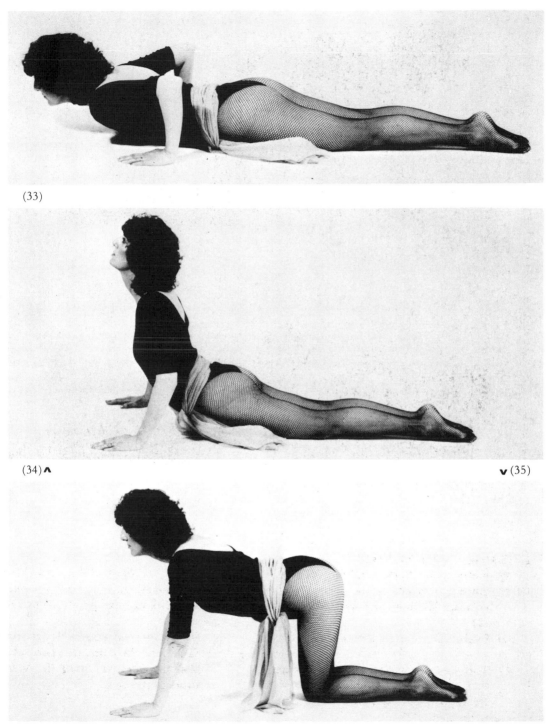

(33)

(34) ∧ ∨ (35)

(36)

Neck and shoulder exercises

EXERCISE 24 – FOR THE NECK

For this next set of exercises you may prefer to sit down, as you may experience a little dizziness if you do it while standing.

(a) Slowly drop your head forward (38), chin on chest. Raise it (39), then drop it back (40) gently – raise, drop again. Repeat several times.

(37)

EXERCISE 23 – FOR THIGHS AND ABDOMEN

This is a very strenuous exercise. Don't try to lean back too far in the initial stages. Do it gradually.

(a) Kneel on the floor, buttocks raised.
(b) Place your hands lightly on your thighs (36).
(c) Keeping your body rigid, slowly sway back as far as you can (37), retaining your balance.
(d) Slowly come back up. Repeat four or five times.

(b) Keeping shoulders level, lower your head towards your right shoulder (41). Raise your head (42), then lower it towards your left shoulder (43), raise. Repeat several times.

(c) Lower your head forward, chin on chest (44). Now in one continuous movement roll your head to the right (45). Around to the back (46) – being careful not to let it drop back too far – then round to the left (47), and forward, completing a circular movement with your head. Do three to the right, then three to the left.

(d) Stretch the neck and chin forward, pulling your bottom lip up and over the top lip. Relax and repeat several times.

(39)

(38)

(40)

(41)

(42)

(43)

(44)

(45)

(46)

(47)

(48) ∧

∨ (50)

(49)

EXERCISE 25 – FOR THE SHOULDERS

The following exercises should help to alleviate tension, which tends to start at the base of the neck, and also to improve bad posture. Unless otherwise stated, the exercises can be done sitting down with the arms relaxed on your lap.

(a) Slowly raise your right shoulder as high as you can (48), then lower (49). Slowly raise your left shoulder (50) as high as you can, then lower. Do this exercise several times, then relax.

(b) Raise both shoulders as high as you can (51), hold, count to four, then relax, lowering the shoulders (52). Repeat several times.

(c) Bring both shoulders forward as far as you can (53), then pull both shoulders back, pushing the chest out (54). Relax the shoulders. Repeat several times.

(51) ∧

(52) ∧

∨ (53)

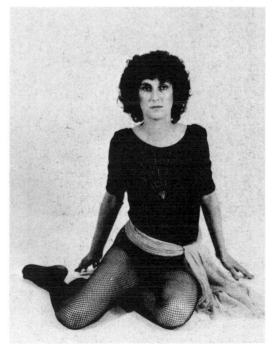

∨ (54)

(55)

(56)

(d) Stand with your feet slightly apart. Elevate the rib cage. Place your hands on your shoulders so that the elbows are out to the side, level with your shoulders (55). Bring both your elbows forward (56), down and up to the back (57), and round to the sides (58). Repeat, doing several circular movements with the elbows.

(e) Stand with your feet slightly apart. Elevate the rib cage. Hold your arms, palms facing upwards, out to the side at shoulder level (59). Keeping them straight, very slowly lift your arms until they are extended above your head (60). Pause, then very slowly bring your arms down to the side again. Repeat several times.

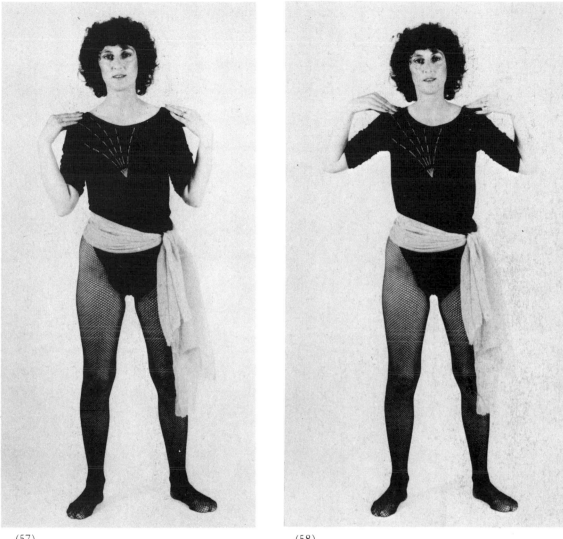

(57)   (58)

(59)

(60)

Supplementary rib cage exercises

These exercises can also be incorporated in a dance.

EXERCISE 26 – RIB CAGE LIFT
slow to medium tempo

(a) Assume the starting position.
(b) Stand with your feet together, knees flexed. Push your bottom out a little.
(c) Hold your arms out to the front at waist level, palms facing upwards, or out to the side, wrists turned upwards.
(d) Lift your rib cage up, but do not raise or pull back your shoulders
(e) Lower your rib cage. Repeat several times.

EXERCISE 27 – TRAVELLING RIB CAGE LIFT

(a) Assume the starting position.
(b) Stand with your feet together, knees flexed.
(c) Hold your arms out to the front at waist level, palms facing upwards or out to the side, wrists turned upwards.
(d) As you step forward onto your right foot, place it directly in front of your left foot, raise and lower the rib cage.
(e) As you step forward onto your left foot, place it directly in front of your right foot, raise and lower the rib cage.
(f) Continue travelling forward, raising and lowering your rib cage, until you have perfected the movement.

EXERCISE 28 – RIB CAGE FIGURE-EIGHT
slow to medium tempo

(a) Assume the starting position.
(b) Stand with your feet very slightly apart, knees flexed.
(c) Hold your arms out to the front at waist level, palms facing upwards.
(d) Pull your rib cage over to the right, then push it forward.
(e) Pull your rib cage over to the central position, then pull it back.
(f) Pull your rib cage over to the left, then push it forward.
(g) Pull your rib cage over to the central position, and then pull it back.

You should have now completed a figure-eight with your rib cage. Practice several times, first to the right, then to the left. This figure-eight can also be done travelling forwards, as follows:

(a) As you push your rib cage over to the right, step forward onto your right foot, placing it directly in front of the left foot.
(b) Push your rib cage forward, pull it to the central position, then pull it back.
(c) As you push your rib cage over to the left, step forward onto your left foot, placing it directly in front of the right foot.
(d) Push your rib cage forward, pull it over to the central position, then pull it back, thus completing the figure-eight.
(e) Repeat several times.

BASIC HIP ROTATION
slow to medium tempo

(a) Assume the starting position. Hold your arms out to the side, palms facing up.

(b) Push your right hip out to the right side (1).

(c) Push the pelvis forward as far as you can (2) and roll the hips over to the left(3).

(d) Push the pelvis back to the rear, sticking your bottom out (4) Straightening your knees, roll the hips over to the right (just as you would if using a hula hoop).

(e) Flex the knees and continue pushing the pelvis forward, as in (c) working through to (e).

(f) Rotate the hips several times in a large smooth circle, then repeat, rotating them in the opposite direction.

(1)

(2)

(3)   (4)

To vary the basic hip rotation, do a large circle and then a small circle (making a circle within a circle).

PIVOTTING HIP ROTATION
slow to medium tempo

(a) Assume the starting position.
(b) Place the weight on your left foot and place your right leg out to the side, keeping the leg relaxed.
(c) Circle your hips as in the basic rotation.

(d) As the hip rolls over to the left, keeping the weight on the left foot raise the right foot a little from the floor and take a short step forward on to the right foot.
(e) Push the pelvis back to the rear. As the hip rolls over to the right, pivot slightly on the left foot, turning to the left. Continue the pivotting hip rotation, turning yourself round in a circle to the left.
(f) Repeat the movement, turning to the right.

TRAVELLING HIP ROTATION
slow to medium tempo
  (a) Assume the starting position.
  (b) Throughout the travelling hip rotation the knees should be flexed and the feet close together. Don't raise your heels.
  (c) Rotate your hips in a circular movement as in the basic hip rotation.
  (d) As the hip rolls over to the left, take a very short step forward on to the left foot.
  (e) Push the hip back to the rear, roll your hip over to the right, and take a very short step forward on to the right foot.
  (f) Do several hip rotations travelling forwards.

The same principle is applied travelling backwards: hip to the right, step back onto right foot; hip to the left, step back on to left foot.

UNDULATING HIP ROTATION
slow to medium tempo
  (a) Assume the starting position.
  (b) Rotate your hips in a large circular movement, as in the basic hip rotation (in either direction), slowly bending the knees.
  (c) Continuing to bend the knees, complete a second hip rotation.
  (d) Without pausing, do two more hip rotations, coming up slowly, and straightening the knees.
  (e) Repeat the movement from (b) to (d).

To vary the movement, do a circle within a circle, i.e. one large hip rotation, then a smaller hip rotation.

Routine 1:
HIP ROTATIONS
slow to medium tempo
Combine hip rotations in the following routine, keeping your transitions smooth and in time to the music.
  (a) Assume the starting position, arms held out to the side or in front, palms facing up.
  (b) *To start*
       8 hip rotations on the spot, varying with large and small rotations.
       8 undulating hip rotations
       8 pivotting hip rotations turning to the left
  (c) *Stepping on to the right foot*
       4 hip rotations, travelling forwards
       4 hip rotations, travelling backwards
  (d) Repeat the routine several times.

THE FIGURE EIGHT
slow or medium tempo
  (a) Assume the starting position.
  (b) Push the right hip forward at an angle, so that it is positioned over the right knee (5).
  (c) Pull the right hip back. Then push the left hip forward at an angle so that it is positioned over the left knee (6).
  (d) Pull the left hip back. Then continue as from (b), tracing a figure eight with your hips several times.
  (e) Repeat, pushing the left hip forward first.

PELVIC ROLL
slow to medium tempo
  (a) Assume the starting position, arms held out to the side, palms facing upwards.
  (b) Thrust the pelvis forward as far as you can.
  (c) Roll the pelvis over to the right, flexing the right knee and raising the heel of the left foot.
  (d) Holding this position, thrust the pelvis forward again. Roll the pelvis over to the left, flexing the left knee and raising the heel of the right foot.
  (e) Repeat several times, rolling the pelvis from right to left and left to right, tracing a half-circular movement.

(5)

(6)

TRAVELLING PELVIC ROLL
slow to medium tempo
  (a) Assume the starting position, arms
      out to the side, palms facing upwards.
  (b) Take a short step forward on to your
      right foot. Thrust the pelvis forward,
      and roll it to the right, pushing the hip
      out to the side.
  (c) As you step forward on to your left
      foot, transferring your weight on to
      the left foot, thrust the pelvis forward,
      and roll it from right to left – making
      an arc – and push the hip out to the
      left.
  (d) Step forward on to your right foot,
      transferring your weight on to your

right foot. Thrust the pelvis forward,
rolling it from left to right and pushing
the hip out to the right.
  (e) Repeat several times, travelling
      forward.

Routine 2:
FIGURE EIGHTS AND PELVIC ROLLS
slow to medium tempo
  (a) Assume the starting position.
  (b) Do 4 figure eights, pushing forward
      with the right hip first, and 4 figure
      eights in reverse, pushing forward
      with the left hip.

(c) Follow by 4 pelvic rolls on the spot, going from right to left.

(d) Step on to the left foot, and travelling forward, continue with 8 pelvic rolls.

(e) Complete the exercise with 8 pelvic rolls, stepping back on to the left foot.

(f) Repeat the routine from (a) to (e).

When you feel competent, put Routines 1 and 2 together, to music, beginning with the hip rotations, keeping your transitions smooth and movements subtle.

THE PELVIC TILT
medium to fast tempo

The pelvic tilt is a primitive dance step that leaves little to the imagination. It is essential to perfect this titillating movement, used extensively in belly dancing, until you can tilt your pelvis forward and backward smoothly and effortlessly.

(a) Assume the starting position.

(b) Tighten your buttocks, thrust the pelvis forwards and tilt upward (7).

(c) Relax the buttocks and push back (8).

(d) Again tighten your buttocks, thrust the pelvis forward and tilt upward.

(e) Relax buttocks, push the pelvis back.

(f) Repeat several times.

PELVIC TILT, TRAVELLING FORWARD

(a) Assume the starting position. Stand with knees flexed, feet close together, arms held out to the side with palms facing upwards.

(b) Take a short step forward on to the right foot. Tilt the pelvis forward twice.

(c) When the pelvis is tilted forward, on the second thrust take a short step forward on to the left foot.

(d) Continue travelling forwards.

(7)

PELVIC TILT, TRAVELLING BACKWARD

(a) Step back on to the right foot, tilt the pelvis forward twice. When the pelvis is tilted forward for the second time, step back on to the left foot.

(b) Stepping back on to the right foot, continue travelling backwards.

UNDULATING PELVIC TILT
medium to fast tempo

(a) Assume the starting position.

(b) Slowly bending the knees, do four pelvic tilts.

(c) Do four pelvic tilts as you come up, straightening the knees.

(d) Repeat.

(8)

(9) ∧

∨ (10)

CAMEL ROCK
medium tempo

The basic step is done by shifting the weight from one leg to the other, in a rocking motion.

(a) Assume the starting position.

(b) Place the weight on your left foot, point your right foot in front (9).

(c) Spring forward lightly on to the right foot, shifting your weight on to your right foot, simultaneously contracting the abdomen and arching your back slightly (10).

(d) Step back on to the ball of the left foot, raising the right foot off the floor, simultaneously relaxing the abdomen and tilting the pelvis forward and up.

(e) Continue the camel rock, travelling forward, leading with your right leg. Then repeat, leading with your left leg.

If you find this step difficult to begin with, omit the contraction of the abdomen and the tilting of the pelvis until you have accomplished the basic footwork. Don't lift your feet too high. The camel rock is a very effective, graceful, flowing movement, which can be done travelling forwards, backwards, sideways, and with quarter turns.

CAMEL ROCK, TRAVELLING TO THE SIDE
medium tempo

(a) Assume the starting position.

(b) Travelling to the right:
Turn your body slightly off-centre, to the right, leading with your right leg. Proceed with the camel rock, travelling to the right, doing four in all.

(c) Travelling to the left:
Having completed your fourth step to the right, the weight should be on your right foot, your left foot slightly raised off the floor. Turn your body slightly off-centre to the left, springing on to your left foot. Proceed with the camel rock, travelling to the left, doing four in all.

(d) Repeat until your transitions are smooth.

THE PELVIC ROCK
slow, medium and fast tempo

(a) Assume the starting position.

(b) Place the right foot forward, the knee flexed, keeping both feet flat on the floor.

(c) Do four pelvic tilts, swaying forward, bending the right knee, and transferring the weight on to your right leg.

(d) Sway back, doing four more pelvic tilts, bending the left knee and transferring the weight on to your left leg.

(e) Continue swaying back and forth, then repeat, placing the left foot forward.

(f) As you sway forward bring your arms out to the front, palms facing upwards.

(g) As you sway back, turn palms over, bringing arms down and out to the back.

(h) Turn palms upwards, bringing your arms forward again as you continue the pelvic rock.

THE CAMEL ROLL
slow to medium tempo

(a) Assume the starting position, and keep your knees flexed throughout the movement.

(b) As you step forward on to your right foot, contract your abdomen and push your pelvis back.

(c) Immediately relax your abdomen and push your pelvis forward and up, completing a smooth rocking motion of the hips.

(d) As you step forward on to your left foot, contract your abdomen, and pushing your pelvis back, immediately relax your abdomen and push the pelvis forward and up.

(e) Repeat several times.

While doing the camel roll, you can move your arms as follows:

(a) Place your left hand near your temple and place your right arm out in front of you, just below shoulder level.

(b) As you step forward on to your left foot, change the position of your arms so that the right hand is by your temple and the left arm is out in front of you, just below shoulder level.

(c) Repeat.

(11)

Routine 3:
PELVIC TILTS AND CAMEL ROCKS
medium tempo

(a) 8 pelvic tilts on the spot, followed by 8 undulating pelvic tilts:
4 travelling forward starting with the right foot, and 4 travelling backward stepping back on to the left foot.

(b) Place the right foot forward and do 4 pelvic tilts (as in pelvic rock), swaying forward, and 4 pelvic tilts, swaying back.

(c) Place the left foot forward and do 4 pelvic tilts, swaying forward, and 4 pelvic tilts, swaying back.

(d) 4 camel rocks travelling forward, leading with the right foot, then 4 camel rocks travelling back, stepping back on to the left foot.

(e) 4 camel rocks travelling to the right, leading with the right foot, then
4 camel rocks travelling to the left, leading with the left foot.

(f) 4 camel rocks in quarter turns, leading with the right foot and turning to the right
4 camel rocks in quarter turns, leading with the left foot and turning to the left.

BASIC HIP THRUST
medium to fast tempo

(a) Assume the starting position. Stand with your feet close together, knees well flexed.

(b) Raise the heel of the right foot. Using the ball of the right foot as a lever, push your right hip out and up (11).

(c) Lower the heel, pulling the hip down and away from the rib cage.

(d) Repeat this movement several times on the right side, and then on the left side.

ALTERNATE HIP THRUST
medium to fast tempo

(a) Assume the starting position. Stand with your feet close together, knees well flexed.

(b) Raise the heel of the right foot, placing the weight on the left leg.

(c) Using the ball of the right foot as a lever, push the right hip out and up.

(d) Lower the right heel, pulling the hip down and away from the rib cage.

(e) Transfer the weight on to the right leg and raise the heel of the left foot. Using the ball of the left foot as a lever, push the left hip out and up.

With practice, you should achieve an even, alternate swinging movement of the hips, to a lively tempo.

(12)

(13)

TRAVELLING HIP THRUST
medium tempo

(a) Assume the starting position.

(b) Take a step forward on to the ball of the right foot and thrust your right hip out and up (12).

(c) Step on to the right foot, lowering the heel, pulling the hip down and away from the rib cage (13).

(d) Step forward on to the ball of the left foot and thrust your left hip out and up.

(e) Step on to the left foot, lowering the heel, pulling the hip down and away from the rib cage, and step forward on

to the ball of the right foot. Continue travelling forward.

(f) Arms: raise both arms, with elbows rounded, above your head. As you step forward with the right foot, stretch your right arm. As you step forward with the left foot, stretch the left arm.

PIVOTTING HIP THRUST
medium to fast tempo

(a) Assume the starting position, arms held out to the side or extended above the head in the Turkish pose (see p. 64).

(14)

(15)

(b) Place the weight on the left leg, knee slightly flexed. Place the right foot forward with the heel raised, knee flexed (14).

(c) Using the ball of the foot, push the right foot slightly up from the floor, at the same time thrusting the right hip out and up (15). As you lower the right foot to the floor, pivot a little on the left foot, turning to the left.

(d) Lower the right foot on to the floor. Keeping the heel raised, immediately push the foot up from the floor, using the ball of the foot, at the same time thrusting the right hip out and up.

Pivot a little on the left foot, turning to the left.

(e) Repeat the pivotting hip thrust several times, turning to the left and then to the right.

(f) When turning to the right, use the right foot to pivot on and the ball of the left foot to push the left hip out and up.

To vary the dance step – having gained confidence in balance and co-ordination – lean back from the pelvis as you pivot round, or do a shoulder shimmy.

(16)

PIVOTTING HIP SWING
slow to medium tempo
   (a) Assume the starting position.
   (b) Keep the weight on the left leg, knee
        flexed. Place the right foot forward,
        heel raised.
   (c) Using the ball of the right foot, push
        up from the floor, thrusting the right
        hip out (16).
   (d) Swing the right leg and hip back,
        placing the ball of the foot on the floor
        behind you. Push your right hip out
        and pivot just a fraction on the left
        foot, turning to the left (17).
   (e) Swing the right leg and hip forward on
        to the ball of the foot. Push up from
        the floor, thrusting the right hip out.
        Then swing the right leg and hip back,
        placing the ball of the foot on the floor

behind you. Thrust the hip out and
pivot again to the left.
   (f) Continue to travel to the left. Repeat,
        travelling to the right, swinging the
        left leg and hip forward and back, and
        pivotting on your right foot.

THE HEEL HIP THRUST
medium to fast tempo
The heel hip thrust is done to a count of
three.
   (a) Assume the starting position, feet
        approximately 75 mm (3 inches)
        apart, knees flexed, arms held out to
        the side.
   (b) One: raise the right foot, leaving the
        heel on the floor.

(17)

(c) Two: while your right foot is in that position, raise and immediately lower the heel of the left foot.

(d) Three: place the right foot flat on the floor beside the left foot. Then raise the left foot, leaving the heel on the floor. While your left foot is in that position, raise and immediately lower the heel of the right foot. Place the left foot on the floor beside the right foot.

When you have accomplished the basic step, include the hip thrust as follows:

(e) When you raise the right foot leaving the heel on the floor, push the right hip out and up. Holding that position, raise and immediately lower the heel of the left foot. Place the right foot flat on the floor beside the left foot.

(f) Repeat on each alternate side.

This is a bouncy, lively step, danced slowly or very quickly, and performed on the spot or travelling forward or backward, but it needs much concentration to perfect.

ARABIC WALK
medium tempo

(a) Assume the starting position.

(b) Step forward onto your right foot – step back onto your right foot – step forward onto your right foot.

(c) Transferring your weight onto your right foot, step forward onto the ball of your left foot and push your hip out and forward.

(d) Step forward onto your left foot – step back onto your left foot – step forward onto your left foot.

(e) Transferring your weight onto your left foot, step forward onto the ball of your right foot and push your hip out and forward.

(f) This step should be done to a four-time rhythm. It will help you if you count as follows: a – 1 and 2 and 3 and 4.

While doing the arabic walk, you can move your arms as follows:

(a) Position your left hand by your temple and your right arm out in front of you just below shoulder level.

(b) With each change of step change the position of your arms.

THE SHIMMY
slow to very fast tempo

The shimmy is a difficult movement to achieve, but it is fun to learn. Done correctly, it is a very titillating and exciting movement which can be combined with many other routine steps in belly dancing. There are three basic movements – the thigh shimmy, the hip shimmy, and the shoulder shimmy.

Thigh shimmy

(a) Assume the starting position, arms held out to the side, palms up.

(b) Feet together, flex knees.

(c) Alternately contract and relax the thigh muscles. Start slowly, working up to a fast tempo.

Hip shimmy
slow to fast tempo

(a) Assume the starting position, arms held out to the side, palms up.

(b) Gently move the right hip forward. As you pull the right hip back, move the left hip forward.

(c) Continue alternating the hips forwards and backwards, starting slowly and working up to a fast tempo. You will soon be shimmying your hips without any effort.

Shoulder shimmy
slow to fast tempo

(a) Assume the starting position, arms held out to the side at waist level, palms up.

(b) Gently move the right shoulder

forward. As you bring the shoulder back, move the left shoulder forward.

(c) Continue alternating the shoulders backwards and forwards, starting slowly and working up to a fast tempo.

(d) Do not hunch your shoulders or tense your arms. You may find this difficult at first, but with practice you will relax.

(e) Do not shake the bust, as this will make the shimmy look coarse. Keep the movement subtle and sensuous.

BASIC SHIMMY
slow to fast tempo

Once you have mastered the hip shimmy and shoulder shimmy, try doing both together, starting gently and gradually working up to a fast tempo.

UNDULATING SHIMMY
medium tempo

(a) With your feet slightly apart, continue to shimmy, bending your knees as much as possible.

(b) Come up, still shimmying. Continue the movements up and down, keeping your back straight and arms steady.

TRAVELLING SHIMMY
medium tempo

(a) Arms held out in front, palms up.

(b) As you shimmy both hips and shoulders, take small alternate steps, travelling forwards.

(c) Now try the same movement travelling backwards.

SIDE SHIMMY
medium tempo

(a) Arms held out to the side, palms up.

(b) Stand with your feet well apart, distributing the weight evenly on both legs.

(c) As you shimmy both hips and shoulders, sway to the right, flexing

the right knee, straightening the left leg, and raising the heel of the left foot.

(d) Continuing the shimmy, sway to the left, flexing the left knee, straightening the right leg, and raising the heel of the right foot.

BACKBEND SHIMMY
slow to medium tempo

This movement is for the more advanced belly dancers only, as it needs concentration, co-ordination, flexibility and balance.

(a) Stand with feet well apart, knees flexed, arms held out to the side, palms up.

(b) Gently shimmy both hips and shoulders, at the same time arching your back and swaying backwards as far as you can. Without pausing, shimmy back to an upright position.

HIP WALTZ
medium tempo

This is a lively, lilting step, combined with a gentle swaying motion of the hips from side to side, which can be done travelling forwards, backwards, on the spot, or with quarter turns.

(a) Assume the starting position, arms out to the side, weight on the left foot.

(b) Step to the side on to the left foot, flexing the knee.

(c) Come up on to the ball of the left foot, then up on to the ball of the right foot.

(d) You should now be up on the balls of both feet.

(e) Raise the left leg out to the side but not too high, placing your weight on the ball of your right foot just for a second.

(f) Then spring lightly on to the left foot, flexing the knee. Keeping the heel down, come up on to the ball of the right foot, then come up on to the ball of the left foot.

(g) Raise the right leg out to the side. Spring on to the right leg, flexing the knee, coming up on to the ball of the left foot, and then up on to the ball of the right foot.

(h) Continue as in (e) and (f).

(i) Eventually you should be able to sway your hips gently from side to side:
springing on to the right leg, push the right hip out;
up on the ball of the left foot, push the left hip out;
up on the ball of the right foot, push the right hip out;
springing on to the left leg, push the left hip out.

SPINNING
slow to fast tempo

Spinning is a lovely way to begin or end a dance routine. It is also very effective if you hold your skirt out to the side, or use a veil.

(a) Assume the starting position, hold the left arm out to the side, the right arm slightly curved across the front of you at chest level.

(b) Starting with your right foot, step a few inches out to the right, turn to the right, pivotting on the ball of the right foot, swinging your arm out to the side. Bring the left leg round, making a complete circle with the weight on your left foot.

(c) Bring your right arm across the front at chest level. Spin, stepping out on to the right foot.

THE HIP SKIP
medium to fast tempo

This advanced step is a very lively skipping step done to a 4/4 tempo, and looks most effective if you hold your skirt out to the side by the right and left hand corners of the back panel.

(a) Assume the starting position, feet together.

(b) Place the weight on the left leg.

(c) Skip forward on to the right leg. Hop on the right leg and swing the left leg forward, contract the abdomen, tilting the pelvis up. Hop on the right leg. Then swing the left leg back, relaxing the abdomen.

(d) Bring the left foot to the side of the right foot, tapping the floor with the ball of the foot.

(e) Now skip forward on to the left foot. Hop on the left leg and swing the right leg forward, contracting the abdomen, tilting the pelvis up. Hop on the left leg. Then swing the right leg back, relaxing the abdomen.

(f) Bring the right foot to the side of the left foot, tapping the floor with the ball of the foot. Then skip forward on to the right leg.

HEAD SLIDE

The head should move from one side to the other as though it is sliding on your shoulders (18-20). There will only be a little movement at first, but with practice it will become more

(18)

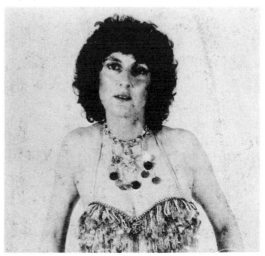

(19)

(20)

exaggerated. It can be done during the descent or ascent of floor movements, or with a veil, as shown in veil techniques. Use a mirror while practising.

(a) Raise your shoulders slightly. Push your chin forward a little.

(b) Hold your hands with palms flat and facing inwards just a few inches away from your ears.

(c) Looking straight ahead, pull jaw and ear to the right and try to touch yor hand with your ear.

(d) Relax and repeat on the left side. When you have mastered the movement you will be able to do it without holding your hands in this position, and they will be free for other movements.

Routine 4:

TRAVELLING HIP THRUSTS
PIVOTTING HIP THRUSTS
PIVOTTING HIP SWINGS
HEEL HIP THRUSTS
HIP WALTZ STEPS
HEAD SLIDES
SHIMMY
medium to fast tempo

(a) 12 travelling hip thrusts, starting with the right foot, moving in a large circle round the floor.

(b) 16 pivotting hip thrusts turning to the left (pivotting on the left foot).

(c) Place the weight on your right foot, and turning to the right do 4 pivotting hip swings, followed by 8 heel hip thrusts on the spot, starting with the left foot.

(d) 4 hip waltz steps, starting with the left foot and, without pausing, do 4 hip waltz steps, travelling forwards, and 4 travelling backwards.

(e) Place the left foot forward, bending both knees, and do 4 head slides.

(f) Place the right foot forward, bending both knees, and do 4 more head slides.

(g) Shimmy round the floor.

5 *Arm Movements*

When dancing never allow yourself to neglect your arms. Don't hold them stiffly or drop them to your sides. Express the mood of your dancing through your arm movements, keeping them soft, flowing and snakelike, enhancing the undulating movements of your hips, and at all times complementing the line of your body movements.

The arm movements start either from the shoulders, elbows or wrists, held either at waist, shoulder or chest level, or extended above your head.

If you suffer from stiffness in your joints, the following movements are excellent exercises.

Group your fingers as illustrated (1), with the middle finger and thumb forward. Don't hold the fingers stiffly or bunched together. The hands should always be graceful and completely relaxed.

For arm movements other than the following, refer to the illustrations of dance steps in Chapter 4.

(1)

(2)

SNAKE ARM ROLL

(a) Assume the starting position.

(b) Extend the arms out in front of you at chest level, elbows very slightly rounded.

(c) Turn the palm of the right hand upwards, the palm of the left hand downwards (1).

(d) Beginning the movement from the elbows, slowly turn both arms over, reversing the position of the palms, then turn back again.

(e) Repeat several times, keeping a continuous soft rolling motion of the arms.

Try this arm movement with hip rotations, figure-eights, or the pelvic roll.

THE COBRA

(a) Assume the starting position.

(b) Hold the arms out to the side at waist level, bend the elbows.

(c) Turn the right arm round so that the palm faces upwards, and the left arm round so the palm faces downwards (2).

(d) Moving only from the elbows, simultaneously reverse the position of the arms (3) so that the palm of the left hand is facing upwards and the palm of the right hand is facing downwards.

(e) Repeat several times.

Try hip thrusts or the abdominal roll with this arm movement.

CIRCULAR ARM MOVEMENT

(a) Assume the starting position.

(b) Hold your arms out to the side, both palms facing downwards (4).

(c) Beginning the movement from the shoulders, bring the arms forward (5) and down (6), swing to the back (7), up and round so that they are now out to the side, having completed a large circle.

(d) Turn the arms over so that the palms face upwards, then over again so that they face downwards. Continue with another soft, flowing circular movement.

(e) Repeat several times, then reverse the arm movement, taking the arms back first.

Try co-ordinating this arm movement with hip rotations, figure-eights and pelvic rolls.

THE RIPPLE

(a) Assume the starting position.

(b) Hold the arms out to the side at waist level, the left arm lower than the right, and the palms facing downwards.

(c) As you raise the left arm and shoulder, lower the right. Then raise the right arm and shoulder and lower the left.

(d) Continue to lower and raise the arms alternately in a soft rippling motion, never raising them above shoulder level.

(3)

(4)

(5)

EASTERN PROMISE

(a) Assume the starting position.

(b) Extend your right arm above your head, slightly rounded, with the palm of the hand facing inwards. Hold the

(6)

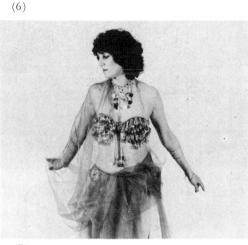

(7)

(8)

(9)

left arm out to the side just above waist level, the palm facing upwards (8).

(c) Simultaneously turn the left arm over so that the palm faces downwards, and turn the right arm round so that the palm is facing outwards (9).

(d) Reverse the position, turning the right arm so that the palm is facing inwards, and the left arm turning the palm upwards.

(e) Repeat several times. Then slowly bring the right arm down and out to the side, extending the left arm above your head. Repeat the arm movement as before.

(10)

(11)

TURKISH POSE
  (a) Assume the starting position.
  (b) Extend your arms above your head, elbows rounded.
  (c) Place the hands back to back, close together. The fingers should be gently curved (10).

This arm position is used when doing the head slide, but it can also be used during other dance steps: the pivotting hip thrust, the alternate hip thrust, the heel hip bounce, hip rotations, abdominal roll, etc.

The zills

The zills are small cymbals which are used to complement the belly dance and the music. They are made of brass or stainless steel and are approximately 5 cm in diameter, with a flat rim and a dished centre. They are positioned on the middle finger and thumb of each hand, just below the nail, and are secured by a strong band of elastic (11). When played, the zills are struck together on the outer rims to create a 'ching' sound. If you strike them face to face, a much duller sound results, with less of a ring to it.

Don't neglect your arm movements when using the zills. Hold the hands as illustrated, keeping the wrists relaxed. If possible, remove the zills before you proceed with the floor movements, since they distract attention from the graceful movement of the hands.

Select carefully the parts of your routine in which you will use the zills. Don't overplay them.

4/4 When counting four time the first and third beats are accentuated, 1-2-3-4, i.e. played louder.

(a)

1	2	3	4
right	left	right	pause
bel	ly	*dance*	–

1	2	3	4
right	left	right	pause
bel	ly	*dance*	–

(b)

1	2 and		3	4
right	left	left	right	left
I	got	no	*rhy*	thm

1	2 and		3	4
right	left	left	right	left
I	got	no	*rhy*	thm

(c)

1	2 and		3	4 and	
right	left	left	right	left	left
I	am	a	*dance*	teach	er

1	2 and		3	4 and	
right	left	left	right	left	left
I	am	a	*dance*	teach	er

(d) 4/4 time played much faster

1 and		2 and		3 and		4 and	
right	left	right	left	right	left	right	left
bel	ly	danc	ing is	is	a	maz	ing

(e) 9/8 This is best thought of as three beats of two clashes, plus one beat of three clashes. Each clash occupies an equal amount of time.

1		2		3		4	
right	left	right	left	right	left	right	left
come	and	*join*	me	*in*	the	*bel*-ly	dance

1	and	2	3	4	5	and	6	7	and	8	9	and
rt	rt	lt	rt	lt	rt	rt	lt	rt	rt	lt	lt	lt
dan-	cing	*is*	*such*	*fun*	*come*	and	*dance*	*come*	and	*dance*	with	me

The veil

There are many ways you can use the veil, which adds an entirely new dimension to the belly dance. It takes considerable practice to co-ordinate the veil and dance steps, but once you have mastered the art, your routine will be transformed into a colourful, seductive and graceful combination of swaying and undulating dance movements, enhanced by the swirling of the veil.

For the veil, select a fabric which is light and soft, such as chiffon or rayon. It should be approximately 2½ metres long, 1 metre wide. If you are short in height, you may need a little less.

Handling the zills with the veil takes a great deal of practice, skill and perseverance.

In the next few pages, I will show you some ways of using the veil. With imagination, by adding your own variations to the basic theme, you will develop your own personal creative touch.

(12)

(13) ∧

∨(14)

HOW TO WEAR THE VEIL

(a) Following the illustrations, drape the veil around your shoulders, making sure the length is equal on both sides (12).

(b) The right side: on the underside, approximately 15 cm in from the far right-hand corner of the veil, using the thumb and index finger of your left hand, pinch a small amount of fabric (13). Bring it up and tuck it down inside your waistband (14).

(c) The left side: drape the veil under the left arm. On the upper side, approximately 15 cm in from the far left-hand corner of the veil, using the thumb and index finger of your right hand, pinch a small amount of fabric (15). Bring it up and tuck it well down inside your waistband (16).

(15) ∧

(17)

∨ (16)

REMOVING THE VEIL

Having made your entrance wearing the veil, you will eventually have to remove it as you dance, without breaking the spell. Follow the instructions until you have perfected the removal of the veil.

(a) Slide your right arm under the veil and, using the thumb and index finger of both hands, take hold of the selvage (the inside edges of the veil) (17).

(b) Pull the veil gently but firmly from the waistband and gracefully move your arms out to the side.

(c) If you have done it correctly, the veil should be hanging down behind you. Make sure it isn't twisted.

(d) Now try removing the veil slowly and gracefully as you dance, keeping to simple movements such as hip rotations and pelvic rolls. Having removed the veil, you are now free to work with it.

(18)

(19)

(20)

Try the following veil movements, combining them with the dance steps:

TWIRLING THE VEIL
 (a) Hold the veil across your front at chest level (18).
 (b) Keeping your right arm straight but not stiff, move it across you towards the left. Then raise it, arching it gracefully behind your head (19).
 (c) Moving to the right, bring your right arm down behind your head, holding it out to the side (20). The veil should now be draped behind you.
 (d) As you bring your right arm down, raise the left arm, arch it gently in

(21)

front of your head (21) and, in one smooth movement, bring your left arm down in front of you (22), and then up and out to the side (23). Continue from (b).

When you have mastered twirling the veil, attempt some basic movements at the same time, such as the hip rotation and figure-eight.

(22)

(23)

(24)

CAMEL ROCK WITH VEIL

(a) Assume the starting position for camel rock.

(b) Drape the veil across your front, your left hand holding the veil on your left hip.

(c) Holding the veil in your right hand, extend your right arm above your head (24). Then, leading with your right foot, proceed with the camel rock.

(d) Keeping the transition smooth as you lead with your left foot, bring your right arm down, holding the veil on your right hip, and extend your left arm above your head. Continue the camel rock.

THE DRAPE

Steps: pivotting hip swing and pivotting hip thrust.

(a) Hold the veil in front of you at chest level and arm's width.

(b) Bring your left arm across at chest level and hold it in that position.

(c) Bring your right arm across the front to the left and up, extending it above your head (25).

(d) Leading with your right foot, proceed with the pivotting hip thrust or pivotting hip swing.

(e) Bring your right arm down and move your left arm over to the left, so that the veil is hanging down in front of you. In one smooth continuous movement, bring your right arm across at chest level, and your left arm across to the right and up, extending it above your head. Continue the dance step, leading with the left foot.

ORIENTAL DRAPE

Step: head slide.

(a) Hold the veil across your front at chest level, arms out to the side.

(b) Hold the veil between your first and middle fingers. Your hands and arms should be on the inside of the veil, and the veil held fairly taut.

(c) Raise your arms up from the side, keeping them straight and extending them above your head. Hold your hands close together, rounding the elbows slightly and draping the veil around your head and shoulders (26).

(d) Now do the head slide.

(e) When changing the position of the veil from the oriental drape to any other veil technique, bring your arms down gracefully to the side and go into your next movement, keeping the transition smooth.

(25)

(26)

(27)

(28)

THE FALL

Steps: travelling hip thrust, pivotting hip thrust, pelvic tilt.

    (a) Hold the veil so that it drapes down behind you, holding your arms out to the side at shoulder level.

    (b) Raise both arms, and extend them behind your head, so that the veil floats behind you. Position your hands close together and back-to-back, keeping the fingers straight (27).

THE FLIPOVER

Step: the pelvic tilt.

    (a) Hold the veil so that it drapes down in front of you at waist level, your arms extended in front but well apart (28).

(29)

(30)

(b) With a sharp flick of the wrists, flip the veil up so that it is draped over the lower part of your arms (keeping hold of the veil) (29).

(c) Flick the wrists, flipping the veil over from the lower part of your arms so that it is draped down in front of you at waist level.

THE BUTTERFLY

Steps: the shimmy, spinning, pivotting hip swing.

(a) With a sharp flick of the wrists, flip the veil up so that the veil is draped over the lower part of your arms.

(b) Raise your arms a little, sliding the veil along your arms towards your shoulders (30), and drape it gracefully round your neck and over your shoulders so that it floats behind you (31).

(c) Take hold of both nearside corners of the veil and extend your arms out to the side at shoulder level, lifting up the veil (32).

This veil movement has a lovely overall effect, particularly when spinning (33).

(31)

(32)

(33)

DISCARDING THE VEIL

As you are coming to the end of the veil routine, drop it gracefully to the floor, making sure that you haven't placed it where you will trip over it or slip on it during the next stage of the dance.

Depending on the audience, you can place the veil round the neck of a friendly spectator!

After discarding the veil, finish off with one or two spins before positioning yourself for the next stage of your belly dance routine.

A COMPLETE VEIL ROUTINE

Wearing the veil, do eight small spins around the floor, and shimmy until you have reached the centre.

Then do four hip rotations from right to left and four from left to right. Follow this with four hip rotations travelling forwards and four travelling backwards.

Travelling round to the right, do four pivotting hip rotations. On the fourth, remove the veil and do four more with the veil draped behind you.

Facing forward, do four hip rotations, twirling the veil above your head. Then swing the veil so that it hangs down behind you, as in the 'fall'.

Do sixteen travelling hip thrusts. On the sixteenth step, position the veil (as in the 'drape') and do four pivotting hip swings. As you complete the fourth, take the left arm to the left hip, extending the right arm.

Travelling to the right, do four camel rocks. Change the position of the veil, and travel to the left, leading with the left foot.

Bring your left arm down, hold the veil in front of you, and position it as in the 'oriental drape'. Do eight head slides.

Bringing your arms down so that the veil is draped in front of you at waist level, do four pelvic tilts, travelling forward. Flip the veil over the lower part of the arms and continue doing four more pelvic tilts.

Then do four pelvic tilts travelling backwards, with the 'butterfly' veil movement.

Shimmy several times.

Finish with eight spins.

6 *Floor Movements*

Floor movements are done to a slow tempo, which imparts to the belly dance a more serious mood.

The body should be lithe, sensuous and snake-like in all movements, with a combination of abdominal rolls, shimmies, pelvic tilts and body undulation.

There are a number of floor movements you will be able to attempt without too much effort, while others will need practice. Don't force yourself − take your time. Floor movements are controlled by the muscles of your thighs and abdomen, and will take time and determination to perfect, but if you feel any strain anywhere − however slight − particularly in your back, rest. Do only a little every day, and your progress and capabilities will surprise you.

THE DESCENT
- (a) Assume the starting position.
- (b) Extend your left leg behind you, with your weight on your right leg (1).
- (c) Bend your right knee. At the same time bend your left knee, sliding your left leg out behind you (2), until the knee touches the floor (3). Bring your right leg back beside your left. You should now be in a kneeling position (4).

(1)

(3) ∧

∨ (4)

(2)

HIP ROTATIONS
slow tempo

   (a) Kneel on the floor, buttocks raised off the floor, keeping the back straight and knees slightly apart. Hold your arms out to the side, the palms of the hands facing upwards.

   (b) Contract the abdomen, elevate the rib cage.

   (c) Do several hip rotations, going from right to left and from left to right in large smooth circular movements.

For variations of the hip rotation from the kneeling position, try the following examples:

(a) Push your pelvis forward, and roll your hips over to the left. As you rotate the hips round to the back, lower the buttocks, brushing by your heels. Raise the buttocks as you roll your hips to the right.

(b) Continue the hip rotation from right to left several times. Then repeat from left to right.

(a) Keeping your buttocks raised and your back straight, rotate your hips in small circular movements, slowly swaying back as far as you can (but don't let your head drop back).

(b) Continue to rotate your hips as you sway back up.

(c) Repeat several times.

(a) As you rotate your hips, lower your buttocks down to your heels.

(b) While continuing to rotate your hips, come up slowly, raising the buttocks.

(c) Repeat several times, rotating the hips from right to left and from left to right.

THE PELVIC TILT
slow to medium tempo

(a) Start in a kneeling position, buttocks raised off the floor, back straight, knees slightly apart, arms out to the side, palms facing upwards.

(b) Contract the abdomen and thighs.

(c) Do several pelvic tilts.

(d) To vary the movement, do four pelvic tilts as you lower your buttocks down to your heels. As you raise them, continue with four more pelvic tilts.

(e) Repeat two or three times.

BODY SNAKE ROLL

(a) From a kneeling position, lower the buttocks and gently sway to the right down on to the right buttock, positioning yourself as illustrated (5).

(b) Elevate the rib cage.

(c) Extend your right arm above your head. Hold the left arm out to the side – but not too high.

(d) Bringing your right arm down, bend over to the right (6). As you move from the right, leading with the right arm and shoulder, stretch forward so that the rib cage is over the right knee.

(e) Lightly brushing the floor with your right arm in a gentle sweeping movement, sway slowly over to the left (7).

(f) Bring your right arm up as you come up from the left, arching the back slightly (8), and continue the circular movement, bringing your right arm down and bending to the right.

(g) Repeat two or three times. Then change position, sitting on your left buttock and bending to the left.

THE FLOOR GLIDE

Stay in the sitting position you held for the body snake roll (5).

(a) Extend your right arm above your head and your left arm to the side.

(b) Elevate the rib cage, contract the abdomen.

(c) Bend forward from your hips, bringing your right arm down so that your rib cage is over your right knee. Keep your left arm out to the side.

(d) Place the fingers of your right hand on the floor in front of you. Gently push your arm forward and stretch until your head touches the floor.

(5)   (6)

(7)

(e) Raise your arm, coming up slowly,
     until your back is straight and your
     right arm extended above your head.
(f) Repeat. Then reverse the position.

(8)

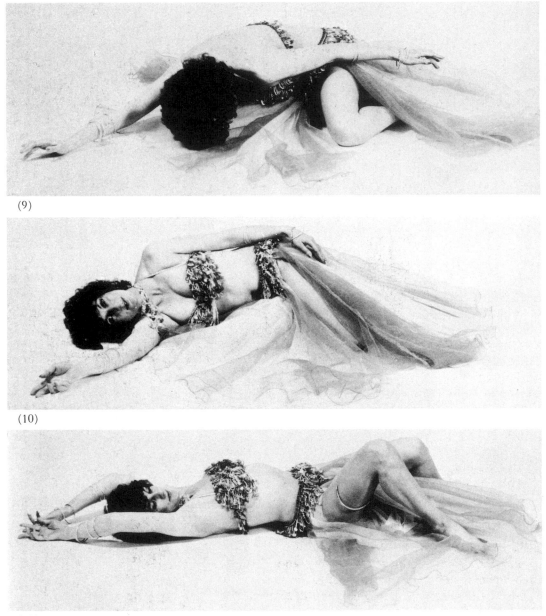

(9)

(10)

(11)

UNDULATING BODY ROLL

Sit in the position you held for the body snake roll (5) and follow the instructions for the floor glide from (a) to (d) and hold. Then continue as follows:

(a) Roll on to your right shoulder, bringing the left arm up so that both arms are on the floor behind you, extended above the head (9-11). The knees should still be in the same

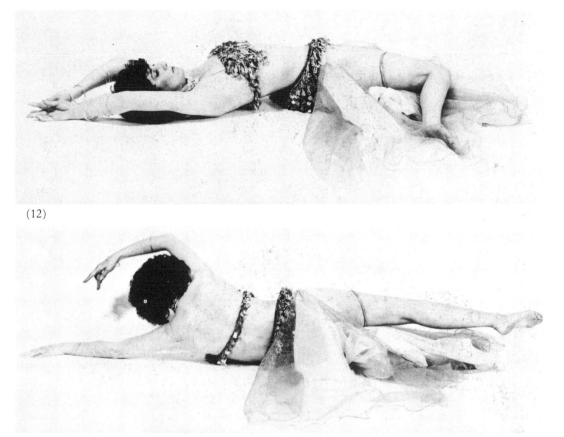

(12)

(13)

(14)

position at this point.

  (b) Continue to roll on to your back. Raise your knees and, keeping them bent, swing them over to the left (12), lowering them to the floor.

(From this position both hips can be raised from the floor, arching the back, and movements such as the abdominal roll, abdominal flutter and hip shimmy can be performed.)

  (c) Roll over on to your left shoulder (13). Using your left hand, push yourself up from the floor, bringing your right arm up above your head (14). You should now be positioned to repeat the movement on the left.

(15) ∧   ∨ (16)

THE BODY LIFT

(a) From a kneeling position, lower the buttocks and gently sway to the left down on to the left buttock.

(b) Elevate the rib cage.

(c) Place the palm of your left hand on the floor beside your left knee, your right hand gently resting on your right leg (15).

(d) Place your weight on your left hand. As you swing your right arm up and over, raise your right buttock, simultaneously straighten your right leg and stretch your body as far over to the left as possible (16). Hold the position for two or three seconds. Do a few abdominal rolls.

(e) As you bring your right arm down, pull your body up from the left. Relax your right leg and lower your right buttock to the floor.

(f) Repeat on the right side.

(g) To vary the movement, do several pelvic tilts as you lift your buttocks. Continue with pelvic tilts as you lower your buttocks to the floor.

(17)

(18)

UNDULATING FLOOR GLIDE WITH SHIMMY

(a) From a kneeling position, stretch your right leg out behind you, so that you are kneeling on the left leg only (17).

(b) Lower your buttocks, tucking your left foot under your left buttock.

(c) Elevate the rib cage.

(d) Keeping your back straight, hold your arms out to the side.

(e) Shimmying your shoulders gently, slowly bend forward until your rib cage is over your left knee (18).

(f) Continuing to shimmy, pull yourself up and repeat the movement two or three times. Then change your position, kneeling on your right leg and straightening your left leg out behind you.

(g) Now try the following combination: kneel on your left leg, stretch your right leg out behind you, bend over to the left, leading with the left arm and shoulder as you come from the left, stretch forward and continue over to the right. Come up from the right, completing a circular movement with the upper part of your body. Shimmy and continue as in (e) – (f).

BACK BENDS

The back bend will take a great deal of practice unless, of course, you are supple and used to more strenuous exercise. It mustn't be rushed as you could injure yourself. Follow the instructions and illustrations carefully in the three stages set out below. You may find it helpful to use one or two cushions or pillows, as these will give your back some support to begin with.

Stage one

(a) Start in a kneeling position, buttocks raised off the floor, back straight.
(b) Contract the abdomen and thighs.
(c) Take hold of your ankles, and slowly arch your back, letting your head drop back as you do so (19). Come up slowly. Repeat two or three times.

Practise this several times until you feel confident and sufficiently stretched to attempt stage two.

Stage two

(a) Start in the same kneeling position as in stage one, and contract the thighs and abdomen.
(b) Take hold of your ankles and slowly bend backwards.
(c) Now slide your hands up to your calves – this should enable you to bend further back.
(d) Repeat two or three times. With practice you will become much more flexible and will be able to attempt stage three.

Stage three

(a) Still in the same kneeling position, slowly bend backwards and place your hands on your calves.
(b) Place the palms of your hands flat on the floor, and as you continue the back bend, slide your arms out to the side, lowering yourself until your head and shoulders touch the floor (20).
(c) To raise yourself from this position, raise your shoulders from the floor and pull yourself up. Or swing your right or left arm across your chest, raising the shoulder, and lift yourself up to a kneeling position.

SHIMMYING BACK BEND

(a) Start in a kneeling position, as in the basic back bend, knees apart, arms out to the side or, if you prefer, extended above your head.
(b) Contract the thighs and abdomen.
(c) Shimmy your shoulders gently.
(d) Keeping up the shimmy, sway back until your head and shoulders touch the floor or, if you prefer, a few inches from the floor.
(e) Come up, still shimmying the shoulders.

As a variation, shimmy back and, while you are in the back position, with the back arched shimmy both your hips and shoulders and come up still shimmying. Or do the basic back bend and include several abdominal rolls before coming up.

(19)

(20)

THE ASCENT
  (a) From a kneeling position, bring your right leg forward, placing your right foot flat on the floor.
  (b) Slowly raise yourself, straightening your left leg, which should be out behind you.
  (c) Bring your left leg beside your right leg. You should now be positioned to do your next dance step.

An effective costume, for practice or performance, consists of four parts – skirt, bra, hipband and veil.

Choose a light material – preferably chiffon. There are many lovely colours and patterns to choose from.

With imagination and your own creative abilities you can design some very erotic and alluring costumes – you will also find it a relaxing and absorbing pastime.

Unless you are performing professionally, it is better to make the simple skirt or harem pants. Not only will they cost less, but they are much easier to move around in and by no means less effective or exotic.

Wearing a costume gives you a tremendous boost. It enhances your movements, and makes you feel more sensuous.

Anything ornamental can be used to decorate the bra and hipband – jewellery, glass beads, bugle beads, old coins, sequins, silver or gold chains, glittery braids, or fringing.

To finish off the outfit, wear a variety of jangly bangles, rings, oriental necklaces and earrings.

Stitch on the decorations securely. Glue them, if you prefer, before stitching. This will lessen the chances of losing them while you are performing.

Full skirt

Use chiffon or fine net curtaining. Sari material is beautiful but very expensive and if you do use it, follow the instructions for the simple skirt, since cutting will ruin the intricate decorative embroidery bordering the fabric. For the full skirt you will need the following:

> six metres of material
> pen or French chalk
> pins
> thread
> scissors
> length of string
> Velcro or hooks and eyes
> curved petersham, enough to go around your hips, allowing approximately 2.5 cm to overlap for fastening.

Follow the instructions and illustrations as follows:

(a) Spread out your length of fabric on the floor and fold the material into three equal layers.

(b) Tie french chalk or a pen on to a length of string long enough to reach the bottom edge of the material. Pin the string to the top end of the material, secure it by pushing the pin into the carpet and draw a large semi-circle as illustrated (p. 88).

(c) At the top end of the fabric draw a semi-circle 26 cm (10 in) across.

(d) Using a sharp pair of scissors cut through all three layers, along the chalked lines. You should now have three separate semi-circles. If you pin all three layers together, it may prevent the material from slipping around while you are cutting.

(e) To form the back of the skirt, sew two of the semi-circles together. Hem all the edges. Hem the front panel, as illustrated.

(f) Place the petersham around your hips and secure it. Using the pen, mark the spots where the skirt panels should reach. The back piece should come round to the front, on either side, just covering the hips. The front piece should hang down the centre.

(g) Gather the waist of both back and front panels. Ease out the gathering. Using the marks on the petersham to position the skirt panels, pin to the petersham and machine. Stitch on Velcro to fasten or, if you prefer, hooks and eyes.

(h) To finish off the top of the skirt in place of a hipband, purchase a required length of sequins on an elasticated backing, or anything else similar, approximately 5 cm deep. Stitch on to the upper band of the skirt.

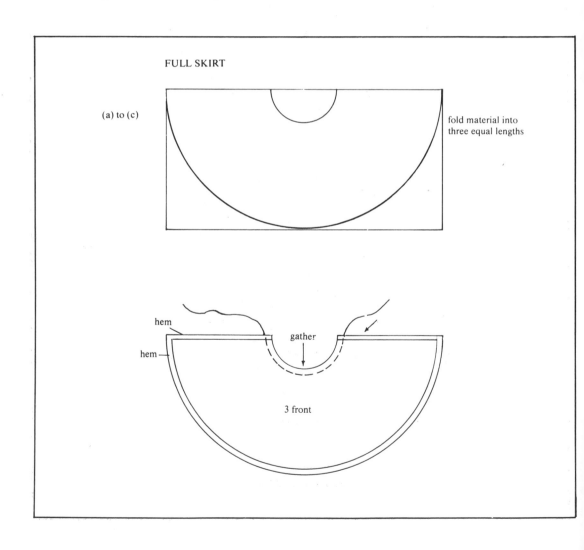

FULL SKIRT

(a) to (c)

fold material into three equal lengths

hem

hem

gather

3 front

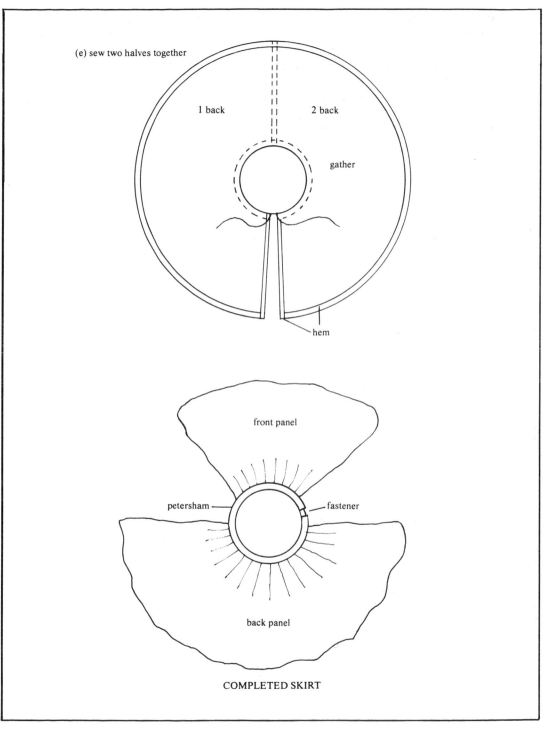

(e) sew two halves together

1 back

2 back

gather

hem

front panel

petersham

fastener

back panel

COMPLETED SKIRT

Simple skirt

This pattern is simple and uses less fabric, but is just as effective as the full skirt. You will need the following:

three metres of material
thread
pins
scissors
Velcro or hooks and eyes

(a) Spread out your length of material. Measure and cut off one metre for the front panel.

(b) Gather along the top edges of the two-metre and one-metre lengths and hem both pieces.

(c) Place the petersham around your hips and secure it. With the pen, mark the spots where the skirt panels should reach. The back piece of the skirt should come round to the front to either side, just covering the hips. The front piece should hang down the centre.

(d) Ease out the gathering of both panels, place and pin on to the curved petersham as for the full skirt and machine.

(e) To fasten the skirt, stitch on Velcro or hooks and eyes.

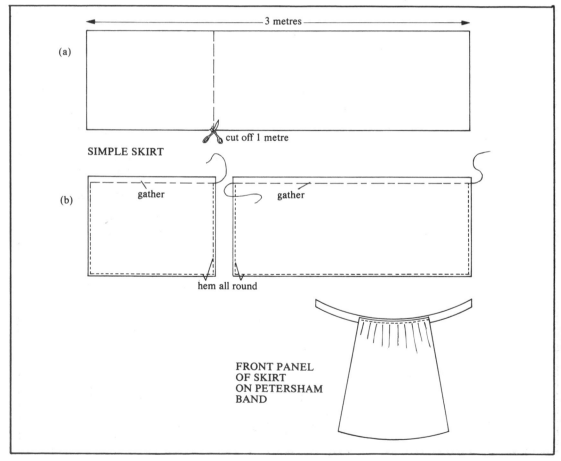

(a)

3 metres

cut off 1 metre

SIMPLE SKIRT

(b)

gather   gather

hem all round

**FRONT PANEL
OF SKIRT
ON PETERSHAM
BAND**

Harem pants

For these you will require:

two metres, approximately one metre wide, of sheer fabric, such as chiffon, any colour, plain or patterned
    thread
    french chalk or pen
    elastic
    scissors
    tape measure

(a) Open out the full length of material and cut it into two equal lengths of one metre.

(b) Double each piece lengthways.

(c) Before drawing the outline and cutting the fabric, take your own measurements carefully. You may need to adjust the measurements slightly from the waistline to the crotch and from the waistline to the ankle. Remember when measuring the outside leg that the waistline is worn below your navel.

(d) Measure, mark and then sketch the outline of the harem pants on the fabric as illustrated.

(e) Using both pieces, cut out two patterns.

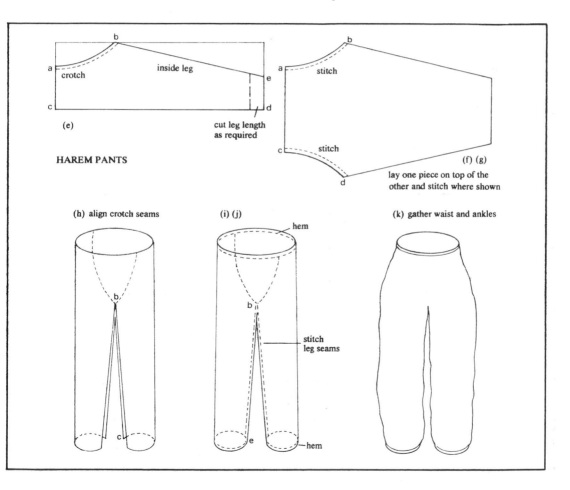

(f) After cutting, unfold each piece and lay one piece on top of the other, making sure that they match exactly.

(g) Stitch to form crotch from *a* to *b* and *c* to *d*.

(h) After stitching, re-arrange the pants so that the crotch seams, both back and front, line up.

(i) Stitch up the inside legs from ankle to crotch, *b* to *e*.

(j) Hem the waistline and leg bottom, allowing enough turning (approximately 25 mm) for threading the elastic through.

(k) Thread elastic through ankles and waistline, gather up to fit.

(l) To decorate, stitch on large or small sequins.

Hip band

For the hip band you will need the following;

a stiff material to fit round hips, approximately 10 cm wide (vilene is excellent to work with)

fabric to cover, preferably the same colour as the skirt

large hooks and eyes, or Velcro

for decoration choose any of the following: jewels, bugle beads, coins, fringing, etc. – dental floss is ideal for stitching and threading beads and can be purchased at most chemists

(a) Measure hips and cut the vilene to size. Shape as you wish or follow the illustrations showing examples of hip bands.

(b) Cover with light fabric.

(c) Plan carefully how you are going to design your hip band, then glue and stitch on securely whatever ornamental pieces you have chosen.

(d) Add hooks and eyes, or Velcro, to fasten.

(e) For variation, make your hip band in two separate pieces, then cut four long lengths of fabric. Hem these all round, then stitch each length onto each side of the hip band. Secure the band around your hips by tying large bows.

The bra

Use a padded bra or one with firm cups; if possible choose a bra the same colour as the skirt or pants. If you wish to keep work to a minimum simply decorate the cups and straps with glittery braid and sequins as illustrated, but do remember that if your straps are elastic you should stretch them as you stitch on sequins or braid.

ALTERNATIVE METHOD

(a) Remove the shoulder straps from the bra and cut out the elastic panels on either side as shown, leaving the strong outer elasticated edge of the bra.

(b) Cover the cups with fabric. Decorate with jewels, beads, coins, sequins or fringing.

(c) Replace the straps with fabric, converting the bra into a halter neck, or position as before. You may find that an all-elastic bra tends to ride up. Use Velcro or hooks and eyes to fasten.

(d) Stitch on sequins or fringing round the sides and back of the bra, remembering to stretch the elastic as you do so.

(e) If desired, you can finish off the bra by sticking on, around the lower edge, colourful dangling lengths of beads or chains, since anything that swings or dangles round the bust and hips accentuates all movement.

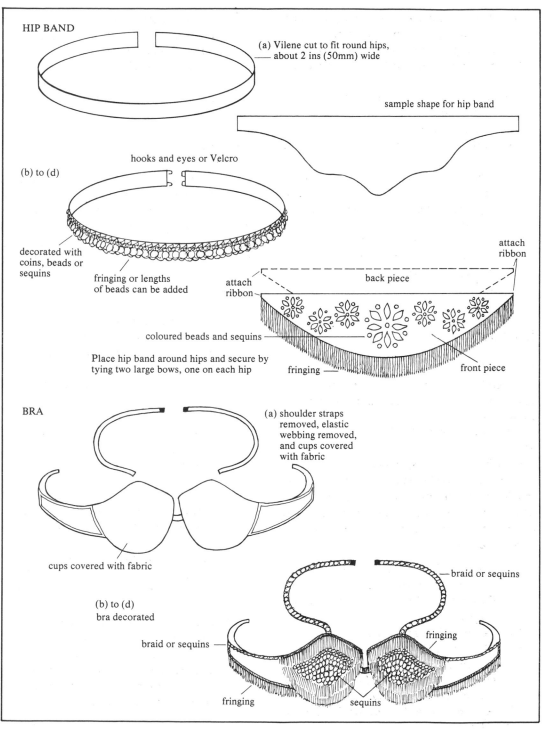

HIP BAND

(a) Vilene cut to fit round hips, about 2 ins (50mm) wide

sample shape for hip band

(b) to (d)

hooks and eyes or Velcro

decorated with coins, beads or sequins

fringing or lengths of beads can be added

attach ribbon

attach ribbon

back piece

coloured beads and sequins

Place hip band around hips and secure by tying two large bows, one on each hip

fringing

front piece

BRA

(a) shoulder straps removed, elastic webbing removed, and cups covered with fabric

cups covered with fabric

(b) to (d) bra decorated

braid or sequins

braid or sequins

fringing

fringing

sequins

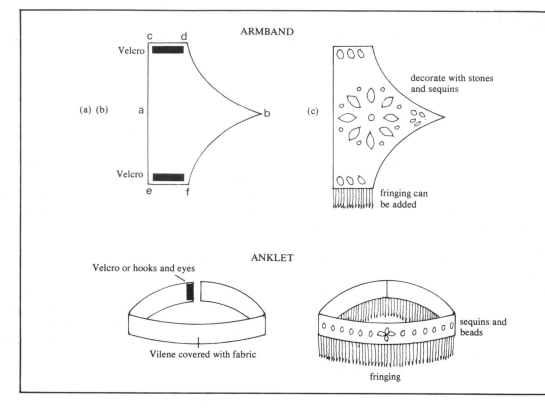

ARMBAND

Velcro

(a) (b)   a

c   d

b

(c)   decorate with stones and sequins

fringing can be added

ANKLET

Velcro or hooks and eyes

Vilene covered with fabric

sequins and beads

fringing

Anklets and armbands

These are worn by many dancers and are a very effective finishing touch to a costume. They are usually covered in the same fabric and colour as the costume, and decorated. You will need the following:

vilene
Velcro
fabric to cover
french chalk
paper
scissors
pins
beads, sequins, fringing, etc.
glue

ARMBANDS
(a) Measure the width to your wrists (c to e). The distance from a to b in the illustration can be varied.
(b) Use a piece of paper and make a paper pattern. Pin it on to the vilene and cut out.
(c) Cover with fabric and sew all round.
(d) Stitch the Velcro on the underside from c to d and e to f.
(e) Decorate with beads, sequins and fringing, etc. To secure, glue on the sequins and beads before stitching.

ANKLETS
Anklets are made in the same way as armbands, but are usually ribbon shaped. The fringing is attached as shown in the illustration.

Conclusion

There is an element of the exhibitionist in all of us and belly dancing, regardless of age or sex, is a wonderful medium for individual interpretation and role playing.

Now that you are thoroughly familiar with all the steps, whether in the privacy of your own home, dancing for friends, or dancing solo as a professional cabaret artiste, this is the moment for you to let your submerged urges take over.

If you wish to perform in public, practice first in front of small groups of people until you have developed confidence and no longer need to plan your movements consciously.

It is more than likely you will suffer from stagefright before a performance, but once you are out there on the dance floor the awareness of your new mental and emotional liberation will enable you to be naturally graceful and fluid, so that your undulating movements combined with the pulsating rhythm of the music will enable your body and mind to derive the greatest possible benefit.

If you make a mistake don't panic – just keep moving and remember to smile.

Above all, whether you take it up seriously or do it just for fun, belly dancing is a unique and exciting way of keeping fit and is a perfect opportunity to create your own fantasies.

So dance on and good luck.

Courses

Evening classes and ten week courses are run by the author in many places, including The Pineapple Dance Centre, Covent Garden, London.

Records

Records of oriental dance music are available from the author.

For details of both courses and records, send a stamped addressed envelope to Tina Hobin, Oriental Dance Scene, 37 The Green, Steventon, Nr Abingdon, Oxon.

Materials for Costumes

Fabrics: Borovick Fabrics Ltd, 16 Berwick St, London W1.
Beads, coins etc.: Ells & Farrier Ltd, 5 Princes St, London W1.

Books

If you have enjoyed this book, there are others you may be interested in too. All the following are obtainable in bookshops, or in case of difficulty direct from the publisher (Duckworth, The Old Piano Factory, 43 Gloucester Crescent, London N.W.1. Tel: 01-485 3484).

FEED YOUR FACE
Dian Dincin Buchman

A complete herbal guide to health and beauty packed with fascinating information about the natural care of hair, skin, eyes, mouth and feet.

ABC OF NATURAL BEAUTY
Dian Dincin Buchman

A convenient handbook, arranged alphabetically, of all the main natural remedies for beauty problems.

GINSENG
Pamela Dixon
In the East the legendary plant ginseng has for thousands of years been regarded as a panacea, valued as an aid to long life, an aphrodisiac and a wonder-working drug. This is the first book to trace its true history from the earliest Chinese herbals to the present day, and to assess its real uses scientifically.

KEEP YOUNG AND BEAUTIFUL
Elinor Glyn & Barbara Cartland
Elinor Glyn's famous book on beauty care, adapted for today's readers by Barbara Cartland, who has added many health and beauty hints of her own based on new scientific facts.